Praise for *The Reality-Based Rules of the Workplace*

"Cy Wakeman's new book is for every member of the workforce who wants to elevate his or her performance to a higher level. *The Reality-Based Rules of the Workplace* provides invaluable tools for converting the energy spent on feelings of frustration, complacency, and hopelessness into fuel for finding happiness and achieving your fullest potential. Cy's philosophy and tools have been invaluable in helping our leaders learn to embrace accountability, and the positive response from employees has been overwhelming."

—**Alyson Guthrie**, chief human resources officer, Crowell & Moring

"One of my biggest disappointments as a CEO is the significant number of good employees we have lost because some incident changed their attitude almost overnight. It is great to finally have a book that helps employees understand how management views them and that they can totally control that perception. The greatest benefit to *The Reality-Based Rules of the Workplace* is that it teaches us all how to be more accountable in our own careers. Every college student should read this to prepare them for the real world and how to thrive in it."

—**Mike Rydin**, president and CEO, HCSS

"In *The Reality-Based Rules of the Workplace*, Cy Wakeman reveals that the key ingredient to both high performance and happiness is simple: personal accountability. With a no-holds-barred approach and practical tools, Wakeman helps employees discover a newfound sense of happiness and control in their work."

—**Kim Ferrarie**, senior vice president, human resources, Air Liquide

"Cy Wakeman's newest book is for every member of the workforce who wants to elevate his or her performance to a higher level of greatness. *The Reality-Based Rules of the Workplace* provides tools for converting any disengagement you are feeling toward your current company into powerful action to re-engage and achieve your fullest potential. We are using Cy's philosophy and tools in our leadership development programs, and the response has been overwhelming! I highly recommend this book if you are ready to challenge yourself to let go of any blockers that are preventing you from being your best."

—**Ken Myers**, senior vice president and chief human resources officer, Hospira, Inc.

"*The Reality-Based Rules of the Workplace* is an essential guide to facing the real challenges you deal with every day and seizing the opportunities they represent, instead of feeling victimized. Cy Wakeman shows how you can adopt a no-nonsense approach to owning your career and becoming the kind of employee no organization would want to lose."

—**Ed Bjurstrom**, general manager, Gilead Sciences

"*The Reality-Based Rules of the Workplace* is spot on! It provides a suite of tangible tools that empower employees to take control of their work life. We all want to determine our own destiny, how we contribute at work, and how we feel about it. This book is key to moving forward! The messages Cy provides are easy to understand and apply across environments."

—**Shannon Bell**, executive coach and organizational development consultant

"If you are an employee or you have employees, *The Reality-Based Rules of the Workplace* is a must-read for thriving in today's marketplace. Cy provides simple steps to developing a culture where employees are contributors and drivers of your basic operating principles, and she provides tips on how to enhance business results by creating relationships that are meaningful and success-filled for employees, coworkers, and your business."

—**Cindy Williams**, organizational development specialist, Bayer CropScience

"*The Reality-Based Rules of the Workplace* is a gem for anyone holding a job, and for those who evaluate the work of other people. Totally engaging, funny at times, and an easy read. This book is packed with questions to ask yourself and guidance toward the best, most productive answers to drive success for yourself, your coworkers, and your business. Cy has hit this one out of the park!"

—**Gordon Whitten**, serial entrepreneur and innovation expert

THE REALITY-BASED RULES OF THE WORKPLACE

Know What
(+) Boosts Your Value,
(−) Kills Your Chances, &
(=) Will Make You Happier

CY WAKEMAN

AUTHOR OF *REALITY-BASED LEADERSHIP*

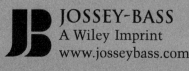
JOSSEY-BASS
A Wiley Imprint
www.josseybass.com

Published by Jossey-Bass
A Wiley Imprint
989 Market Street, San Francisco, CA 94103-1741—www.josseybass.com

Cover design by Faceout Studio

Jossey-Bass books and products are available through most bookstores. To contact Jossey-Bass directly call our Customer Care Department within the U.S. at 800-956-7739, outside the U.S. at 317-572-3986, or fax 317-572-4002.

Wiley also publishes its books in a variety of electronic formats and by print-on-demand. Not all content that is available in standard print versions of this book may appear or be packaged in all book formats. If you have purchased a version of this book that did not include media that is referenced by or accompanies a standard print version, you may request this media by visiting http://booksupport.wiley.com. For more information about Wiley products, visit us www.wiley.com.

Library of Congress Cataloging-in-Publication Data
Wakeman, Cy.
  The reality-based rules of the workplace : know what boosts your value, kills your chances, and will make you happier / Cy Wakeman.—First edition.
     pages cm
  Includes bibliographical references and index.
  ISBN 978-1-118-41368-5 (cloth); ISBN 978-1-118-58555-9 (ebk);
ISBN 978-1-118-58567-2 (ebk); ISBN 978-1-118-58570-2 (ebk)
  1. Success in business. 2. Job satisfaction. 3. Organizational behavior. 4. Office politics. I. Title.
  HF5386.W158 2013
  650.1—dc23
                                                                    2012046244

Printed in the United States of America
FIRST EDITION
HB Printing   10 9 8 7 6 5 4 3

In honor of my incredible dad,
the greatest storyteller on earth.
What I would give for just one more dance . . .

In loving memory of my amazing mom,
who knew all along I would become a teacher.
Thanks for teaching me all the greatest lessons in life
and, "Let's keep thinking, shall we?"

We are called to be architects of the future, not its victims.

—Buckminster Fuller

Contents

Contents

THE
REALITY-BASED
RULES OF THE
WORKPLACE

Introduction
The New Rules of the Game

Every day, those of us lucky enough to be employed march off to work. You know, the place with the atrocious coffee? Where an accidental "Reply all" can keep the rumor mill going for weeks? Where everyone is preoccupied with what they will have for lunch, even though the options rarely change? Where you have endless meetings and three types of colleagues: the geniuses who think like you, the jerks who don't, and the idiots—nice though they may be—who have been promoted past their intelligence? Where you have brainstorming sessions with your bagels, passive aggression with your birthday cake, and where pizza is associated with celebrating big wins in a way that it hasn't been since your Little League days. How's work working for you? I'm going to go out on a limb and guess that it could be better.

The employed have never been less satisfied with their lot. Nearly 68 percent of Americans report that their employers have taken steps such as putting a freeze on hiring or wages; laying off staff; reducing work hours, benefits, or pay; requiring unpaid days off; or increasing work hours.[1] Tough economic times have left fewer people to do the same amount of work. Jobs you used to love have become overwhelming; jobs you never loved have become intolerable. Success seems like an impossible dream as you strive to do more with less. You've seen good people get laid off and you've seen good jobs outsourced to cheaper workers. So many people are confused, complaining, blaming, angry, under-responsible for their own affairs and over-responsible for what isn't within their sphere of influence. Employees have come to believe that suffering is now part of working life, and you are suffering more than ever.

It has become normal for work to suck.

Because I travel to more than two hundred companies per year to work with their employees, I see this dissatisfaction first-hand. Many employees feel unrecognized, under-rewarded, and taken advantage of. They want me to understand the scale has tipped—and not in their favor. Their jobs have officially become undoable by the average human being.

What if you could go to work feeling energetic and excited, regardless of any external circumstances? You could go into work today and have fun, be productive, and return home at peace, with energy left over for your family and friends. You could be valued, appreciated—even a favorite at the office. What if you and your boss were allies, and you loved your job again? What if the things that are currently making you unhappy simply lost their power over you?

All this is possible, and more. How do I know? Because thousands of employees have come into my sessions feeling dejected and undervalued, even hopeless, and left with an entirely new perspective. They have awakened to a different way of approaching their reality. They have become calm, creative, results driven, and reality based. They have been able to influence their colleagues, their bosses, and their teams. They have freed themselves from anxiety and resentment. They have turned their long list of excuses into an even longer list of proud accomplishments and results. Not because they work harder, or are in denial, or have surrendered to the "man," but because they changed their mind-sets.

I am here to tell you: You are not a cog in a machine—far from it. You have more control than you think. That's the good news. The bad news is, you and you alone are causing your own suffering. What most of you have lost touch with is that it isn't your reality that is causing your pain and frustration. It's the worn-out methods, techniques, and mind-sets with which you are approaching your reality. I'm here to tell you that your suffering is optional. I can help you get back on track so you can find bliss in your work again, while becoming more valuable to your organization than ever before.

When you feel vulnerable, even defensive, it's all too easy to blame the economy, political leaders, your boss—everyone except the one person you can control: yourself. You do not have to give up your chance at happiness and fulfillment in the name of productivity. If you tend to your own happiness and get wholehearted in your work, then you will be extremely productive. Your effort will make a difference. What's more, your coworkers and your organization will love you for it. Instead of being resentful and keeping score, you will free your creativity and become a highly valued and sought-after employee.

Your speculation, worry, and perspective on the world are nearly always harsher than your world itself. Unfortunately, imagination plays a huge part in creating that which you fear. You may be stuck in a self-fulfilling prophecy that keeps you in survival mode and holds you back from reaching your true potential. Many of

3

you have become resigned to the idea that happiness depends on what happens to you, when in fact, it is all about what you do. I'll show you how you may be unintentionally sabotaging your own results, how to stop, and how to make sure that the work you do is contributing to the bottom line and being noticed by the people who count. You must not wait for others to improve your quality of life. You have it within you to get what you want. But first, you have to embrace Reality and play by its rules.

The Reality-Based Revolution

Einstein famously said that no problem can be solved from the same level of consciousness that created it. For twenty years, as a consultant to top executives and organizations, I have been teaching people to shift their focus from wishing for their circumstances to change to understanding that the ultimate freedom comes from seeing their circumstances differently, and from that place of neutrality, choosing how they will react to what happens around them.

My first book, *Reality-Based Leadership*, introduced leaders to the attributes they must develop in themselves in order to lead well. In that book, I showed them how to think constructively instead of destructively and surprised them with the news that their best people aren't always who they think they are. They learned why they should "work with the willing," putting most of their effort into cultivating the employees who are truly accountable and produce the best results, when most tend to do the opposite, giving their time and energy away to people who resist their efforts.

After *Reality-Based Leadership* was published, I hoped leaders would be satisfied. For a while, they were. People came up to me at my seminars with dog-eared copies, stuffed with page flags and

4

Post-it notes, which showed me how actively they used the book. Their enthusiasm was catching within their organizations, and I was thrilled to see their results. But soon, they began to tell me there was something missing.

Leaders had worked hard to change their mind-sets and to become Reality Based, having noticed that when they accept and work within certain basic principles, they excel, and when they don't, they end up stressed and exhausted. They had worked on their management style, absorbing the message that they should focus their energy and coaching on their best people. But how did these "best people" that I tell leaders to focus on get to be the best? Was it an accident of birth, a skill certain families imparted and others did not? Unfortunately, no one is born accountable, self-reliant, self-mastered, and resilient, yet these are the qualities that count, the ones that will fill you with confidence and afford you the chance to choose your own destiny, no matter what your field of endeavor. Fortunately, anyone can develop them. But how?

What Happy High-Performers Taught Me

My Reality-Based philosophy has been honed by hard-won, hands-on experience in a variety of arenas, including manufacturing, banking, government, high tech, and health care. I first began to develop it when I was working as a counselor, helping clients overcome their challenges, find happiness, and regain a sense of confidence and efficacy in their lives. For many people, work was a huge source of stress and unhappiness, and I helped them to see that it didn't have to be that way. Work isn't something to dread or survive. It can be a place where you live your passions and truly make a difference.

I went on to study the two types of high performers: the happy high-performer, who reports feeling content and stress-free at work while producing top results, and the unhappy high-performer, who delivers good results but is riddled with stress, full of complaints, and generally dissatisfied. Through extensive interviews with two hundred happy high-performers, some commonalities emerged, most notably, that they reported high levels of engagement, a common measurement of happiness at work.

These curve-breakers had in common the core belief that they each made an impact on their circumstances and could choose their own course—in short, they were highly accountable. They seemed immune to factors that completely derailed others, like change and uncertainty, indifferent or ambivalent leadership, and unpredictability. As I studied them, I realized that the bottom-line value they added at work was high. They gave great performance without drama or excessive demands on those around them. It became clear that their success was not due to superior job opportunities, great bosses, coworkers, or luck. Their companies didn't necessarily give them the tools they needed to do their jobs or anything extra in the way of support. Their attitudes were what set them apart.

So how could more people join their ranks? I surveyed more than fifty thousand employees to investigate the relationship of engagement to accountability. For years I had been hearing that only engaged workers produce top results, so if you want to get top results in an organization, you have to make sure employees are happy. (In other words, remove their obstacles and give them better circumstances. Make their lives easier.) What I found out ran counter to this conventional wisdom. My research showed that the main difference between happy employees and unhappy employees was their own level of accountability, not their circumstances. Accountability was driving both engagement and results. People who were highly accountable were both happier and more successful than others, regardless of their circumstances.

Based on these findings, I began to formulate the Reality-Based Rules of the Workplace—the five rules that will allow you to join the ranks of the happy high-performers. This is the book that leaders have been asking for, and it will show you exactly how to become one of the best, most highly valued members of any team. It will also give you back your life. You may not believe it yet, but by the end of this book I will show you that what works for you is also in the best interests of your company, and vice versa. Work can be joyful and fulfilling as well as productive, and by using Reality-Based techniques to face your challenges, you can turn the job you already have into the job you want. Instead of waiting for someone else to develop your talent, you can take back control and start planning a future that you can contemplate with joy. You'll become immune to the bullying, drama, and attitudes of others. You'll become a favorite at work rather than worrying about who is being favored. You will attract opportunity and come to realize that regardless of your position, power, or place on the organization chart, you have far more influence than you ever knew. You'll stop asking yourself, "Is it worth it?" and start asking, "Am I worth it?" If you follow the Reality-Based Rules, your answer to that question will be a resounding, "Yes."

Know Your Real Worth

If you read *Reality-Based Leadership*, you'll find lots of new ideas and fresh looks at concepts that I first introduced in that book. In *The Reality-Based Rules of the Workplace*, I make my proven approach applicable, not just to managers and team leaders, but to every employee at every level, including job seekers. The biggest difference between the two books is that this book is not about coaching others—it's giving you the tools to coach yourself. These tools will free you from dependence upon anyone else for your own success. The book is organized around a new metric that will do more to help you measure and increase your value at work than any performance review or evaluation: the Employee Value Equation. If you are one of the many people who feel unsure of where they stand at work, or in the job market today, I promise you that by the end of this book you will have clarity. You will know how you measure up in the current realties of the workplace and what your worth can be in the very near future.

Someone once told me, as I prepared to leave my day job to go into business for myself, to think about my decision carefully, because when you are the business owner, you earn exactly what you are worth. To me, that is an extraordinarily empowering concept: to earn what you are worth. To get honest feedback from the marketplace about how you measure up and the amount of value you add. That is what I offer you in this book, risk free. Until now, you have just had a few sources of feedback and a performance review number. I'm going help you arrive at a much more reliable and true measurement of your value and then show you how to maximize it to give, and get, what you are worth.

In just a few short weeks, through a major shift in mind-set and a few new behaviors, you can completely change your own level of happiness and engagement in your current job, with the same boss, and even the same team of coworkers. Happiness is at your fingertips, yours for the taking. All jobs can be great jobs. All bosses can be exactly what you need. You can have success any time, anywhere.

People who take my teaching to heart have told me how it makes them feel. They use words like, *immune, bulletproof, strong,*

8

in control, rejuvenated, sane, and *free.* Reality-Based people are full of confidence about their futures. They are continually in touch with me, telling me how this material has changed their lives both at work and at home.

I receive a lot of responses from people eager to share what has worked for them and hoping to inspire others to try it for themselves. Throughout the book, drawing on experiences from this diverse group, including executives I've coached, employees who have attended my monthly webinars, and people who've approached me after keynotes, I tell stories of people who are out there putting my Rules into practice every day. By reading about a challenge overcome at work; an unforeseen benefit of Reality-Based thinking; a transformative experience; a motivating push in the right direction, you'll get inspiration for your own transformation. In addition, I share some personal stories. In my work with clients, I am always candid about my own flaws and difficulties. We are in this together, and I believe that part of good coaching is being able to admit to struggles and challenges of my own. I was not born with the competencies I teach in my seminars and books—and that's what makes me an effective teacher.

Consider this book your roadmap to the higher ground. In order to get there, you have to start from where you are now, and the first step is measuring your current value. In Part One, I introduce the New Value Equation, a self-assessment tool that will show you where you stand. Just as almost every organization has adopted a core strategy of improving its value in the marketplace to gain market share, win over customers, and sell its products and services profitably, you too must deliver sustainable value at a low total cost. This emphasis on value is driving new conversations and new requirements in all organizations—and requires curve-breaking performance from ready and willing employees on a daily basis. The problem is, by the time these conversations filter down to employees, the message is not as explicit and direct. Employees are profoundly affected by these changes, and you need to know how they affect the ways in which you will be measured, rewarded, and employed in the future. The New Value Equation will give you the ability to calculate your true worth, regardless of economic fluctuations. You can choose to become one of the people that your boss and your company want to invest in, listen to, and promote.

Your true value as an employee is not dependent on larger economic conditions—good or bad. It is based on the value that you bring to your organization, the market value of your work, and the return on investment that you deliver, both economically and emotionally, now and into the future. Nearly all of these factors are within your control. When I work with organizations, many employees tell me their main issue is that they don't feel valued. I share the secret with them—that the fastest way to get valued is to add a ton of value. You must get clear about the value you truly bring to your organization, using the New Value Equation:

Your Value = Current Performance + Future Potential −
3 × Emotional Expensiveness

The three factors that make up your equation—Current Performance, Future Potential, and Emotional Expensiveness are the subjects of Chapters One to Three.

Chapter One answers the question, "How am I doing today?" Most employees are used to getting feedback on their performance in the form of yearly performance reviews. But in many companies, those reviews have lost their meaning, and the connection of your number to your company's success is likely tenuous at best. For many employees it has become a source of distress, and it is not moving individuals toward happiness or organizations toward the results they want. I show you how to cut through the confusion and assess your current performance in a meaningful way.

Chapter Two helps you answer the question, "Am I ready for what's next?" While a lot of lip service is paid to Performance, Future Potential is one factor that not many managers are talking about and even fewer employees are focused on. Your attention has most likely been focused on surviving the present, and that's understandable, because for many, the present feels painful enough without looking ahead to an uncertain future. But the truth is, some of your pain (more than you may think) is the direct result of ignoring your responsibility for—and need to work on—your Future Potential. You must proactively grow—not wait for someone else to develop your potential or tell you what you need to learn—in order to become a high-value contributor.

In Chapter Three, I introduce the third and most crucial factor in the New Value Equation: Emotional Expensiveness. This is a factor that almost no one talks about but everyone senses. It is the single most important factor in the New Value Equation, the one that determines whether our Performance and Potential add anything meaningful to the bottom line, and whether others feel that working with us is worth the effort. When I put a name to this factor, which has long been nameless, there is sometimes an audible sigh of relief. Emotional Expensiveness has a high impact on your rewards and job security even though it is rarely overtly discussed. I'd like to change that and give you words to discuss it and strategies to deal with it.

At the end of Part One, I show you how to calculate your Value Equation so that you can get started. Ideally, you will end up with a positive number, but a zero in this context counts for a lot, because most people I work with start out in the negative digits. No matter what your number is today, on the new playing field, you have a chance to become one of the top people in your organization—a highly credible, valuable, even indispensable employee who delivers results no matter what the circumstances and adapts to change quickly and without drama. The good news is that the same behaviors and mind-sets that will raise your number and add the most value to your company will bring you the ultimate happiness in your life. That is a great discovery. Your happiness is not mutually exclusive to the organization's needs and wants. In fact, they are one and the same.

After you have calculated your value in Part One, I show you how to maximize it, playing by the new rules. In Part Two, I explain the five Reality-Based Rules to live by if you want to increase your happiness and your value dramatically:

Chapter Four: Rule #1. Your level of accountability determines your level of happiness, so *don't hope to be lucky. Choose to be happy.*
Chapter Five: Rule #2. Suffering is optional, so *ditch the drama!*
Chapter Six: Rule #3. Buy-in is not optional. *Your action, not opinion, adds value.*
Chapter Seven: Rule #4. Say "Yes" to what's next. *Change is opportunity.*
Chapter 8: Rule #5. You will always have extenuating circumstances. *Succeed anyway.*

You'll find out what each rule has to offer you and learn strategies to put them into practice. If you work through the exercises in these chapters, and take my message to heart, you will transform your relationship to work forever and for the better. Stress is your wake-up call that you need to adjust your thinking and question your beliefs. Your journey will be straightforward, but not easy. I want you to have the ultimate freedom, not to be beholden or dependent on others, not to let circumstances stop you from doing what you set out to do. You'll spend a minimum of two thousand hours at work this year. You can spend that time feeling insecure, resentful, and at the mercy of ever-changing circumstances beyond your control. Or you can feel peaceful, free, and in charge of your own success. I urge you to embrace Reality, choose freedom, and own your future like never before.

Many of us spend our lives wishing that, for once, it would be "all about me," when the truth is that it really is all about you, but not in exactly the way you might have hoped. A word of warning before we start: I am about to ruin your misery. You will no longer be able to see yourself as an innocent victim of your circumstances, but as their co-creator—a participant, whether active or passive, in everything that is happening in your world. If you want happiness and success in your life, the following pages will show you how to claim it.

The New Value Equation

In Part One, The New Value Equation, I explain the three factors that make up the New Value Equation: Current Performance, Future Potential, and Emotional Expensiveness. These factors will determine how you are measured, retained, and rewarded in the future. I show you how to rate yourself for each factor, then give you some quick ways to improve your ratings. By the end of Part One, you'll know where you stand, what you need to work on to be highly employable in any economy, and why you owe it to yourself to take responsibility for your own fulfillment and development. You own your future. This is where it all starts: your empowerment, your reconnection to your own results, your own value, your own reality, your own truth.

1

Your Current Performance

Performance review time brings excitement and dread in the workplace. Most of you are rated at least once a year. You feel invested in your performance numbers to the extent that they may be tied to incentives like raises and promotions, and who wouldn't want the praise and recognition that you hope to accrue in what could be a rare one-on-one meeting with the boss? The dread comes in because, for many employees, the yearly review is the only time you receive meaningful feedback on your performance, good or bad. You may be nervous about it, and you may sense that your boss is not looking forward to it any more than you are. Performance reviews can be emotionally fraught, and they take up a lot of time and energy that contributes very little to the bottom line, so managers are often tempted to put them off. What's more, they are subject to a lot of common errors, on both sides of the desk, that could be avoided.

In this chapter, I explain what performance reviews—which have been the metric of choice in most businesses for years, and at times your only indication of your value—are meant to do, and why the system isn't working and has in fact become a major point of contention between many employees and their bosses. You'll learn how to answer the question, "How am I doing?" for yourself in a way that is truly meaningful, and boost not only your value and productivity but also your contentment at work. You will find your equanimity, not only at performance review time, but all year long.

Performance Reviews in Theory

Your performance review is meant to show you how you have measured up to expectations at work in the past year and focus your mind on your role in delivering on the organization's goals. It is a chance for you and your supervisor to document and discuss how well you've performed your daily activities and conformed to the behaviors that help the company run smoothly; your success or failure to deliver on goals for the previous year, ideally based on the larger goals of the organization so you know how your work fits into the big picture; your performance rating, your score or "grade" for the year; and your plans for the year ahead.

Each year, you promise your employer a set of deliverables and agree to areas of accountability. Your organization agrees to a price for your services. In order to keep your job, and qualify for raises or other benefits, you need to meet or exceed expectations. Once a year, your work is held up for inspection by your leader, who reviews what you committed to and helps you account for your results. You identify goals you delivered on and any gaps between what you promised and what you achieved. You discuss behaviors that helped or hindered your performance, and at the end of the meeting it should all boil down to a single rating of your work that provides a clear message for you and helps the organization take an inventory of its talent and their performance. The annual review process is meant to provide an objective, nonpersonal, transparent, and up-front view of the value you added over the past twelve months, along with suggestions for growth and behavior changes that would increase your chances of adding value in the future.

In a company where this system is working well, employee performance numbers should be represented by a bell-shaped curve (see Figure 1.1). The majority of employees would be rated as "average" and fall in the middle of the curve. The left-hand tail of the curve would represent those who lagged behind and were rated "below average." The right-hand tail would represent the highest performers, the curve-breakers whose practices should be rewarded and replicated throughout the organization so that, next year, results would improve—in effect, picking that curve up and moving the whole thing to the right. The hope is that, through clear differentiation of performance levels, happiness and satisfaction will increase because everyone will be clear on what is expected of them,

Figure 1.1

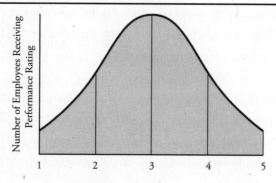

19

Figure 1.2

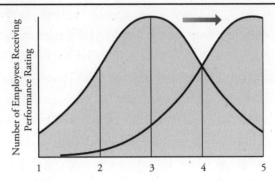

get good feedback on any shortfall, and be rewarded according to his or her contribution (see Figure 1.2).

Wouldn't it be great if that was what actually happened?

Performance Reviews in Reality

Anyone who has ever been through a performance review knows that it is far from the clean and straightforward process it is meant to be. But in order to understand what is going wrong at the individual level, we have to start by looking at the organizational level. The main reason I believe performance reviews as they are used in most companies are an inadequate measure of true value is that they seem to create an alternate reality that is divorced from companies' actual results. In other words, in most organizations there is no correlation between employees' yearly performance ratings and the results that the company is experiencing.

Many times as a leader, and later as a consultant, I have had the experience of hearing, on the same day, two opposing messages within the same organization. From Human Resources, I'd hear that many hardworking and effective employees had delivered results that merited high "exceeds expectations" performance ratings and therefore would receive pay raises. Then the chief executive officer CFO would describe the company's challenging financial outlook and explain how results had fallen far below expectations. I often sat wondering, "How can that be? Top performance by the majority of employees at the same time that results are coming in far below projections? Should we be rewarding this? How will we remain competitive?" There seemed to be a disconnect in many organizations—not just a few. Shouldn't the contributions employees have made add up to results for the company? I went out to study the reality of it, to try to solve the mystery of why this simple math had become so complicated.

I wanted to know how tightly correlated (and therefore how accurate, honest, and true to intent) performance ratings were to organizational results. So I gathered statistics from thirty-seven companies over the course of five years, involving more than 275,000 employees in total. I conducted an audit comparing each company's yearly results with that year's overall performance rating distribution. How were employees' results stacking up by comparison to the company as a whole? In companies where the average employee is assessed as "exceeding expectations," I expected to see great results overall. In companies where the most performance scores were "average" or "below average," I'd have expected to see results that conformed to a lower standard.

What I found was that, in companies where the majority of employees had been rated as "above average" for performance, actual results were 10 percent below industry standards in a variety of categories, including profitability, market share, employee retention, and customer satisfaction. Those companies whose overall performance ratings mapped most closely to a bell-shaped curve over five years, meaning that the majority of employees were rated as "average," and just a few rated as "above" and "below average," achieved far better outcomes year after year.

I found that, in less successful businesses, employees were more likely to be highly rated for performance. In other words, there was a lot of "grade inflation" going on. Within many companies I studied, the performance numbers skewed so high it would appear that they were all claiming to have all the best performers in their industry, which would be impossible. Meanwhile, successful companies were far more likely to rate the employees responsible for their success as "average," that is, delivering as expected, as promised, and as needed to stay competitive.

Sorry to be the one to break the news to you, but in many companies, individual performance reviews have become totally disconnected from results. That's why you can't trust a top rating in your performance review. It tells you very little about where you stand and how much you are contributing to the bottom line, and it doesn't say anything about your Future Potential. One thing is for sure: your performance number is no longer a trustworthy measure of your value or a predictor of results in your organization.

How Performance Reviews Go Wrong

Although my research proves that performance reviews aren't working well for many employees as a measure of value, there are other reasons to take them with a grain of salt.

First, performance reviews are static and retrospective, and they are of a world long past. They only measure how you have performed to the minimum standards of your job. They encourage an unhelpful focus on the past at the expense of the future.

Second, performance reviews compare you to other employees within your company, when in fact your and your company's competition is across your industry as a whole. If you're not being rated against the highest level of professionalism and competence in your field, you're not getting the true measure of your value, either in terms of your career prospects or what it takes for your company to compete in the marketplace.

Third, we tend to confuse effort with results. Your organization gets no return on investment for effort. It is hard for managers to give an employee an average or below-average rating when they know he or she has worked hard, but in reality it is outcomes—not effort—that count, and that is what we all should be measured on. In order to avoid conflict, they have lowered their standards and stopped differentiating, which is the very thing the best employees would like to see more of. In a survey I ran in 2011, 75 percent of employees said the most important motivator for them was to be paid and rewarded according to their actual contribution. So lack of differentiation backfires in both directions. Those of you who are lagging behind are lulled into a false sense of security, and those who are truly stepping up are robbed of the recognition and rewards you deserve.

Both managers and employees tend to personalize Performance Ratings in a way that is unprofessional. These numbers are not—and never have been—a referendum on you and your worthiness as a human being. We must put that aside if we want to have an accurate accounting. But we don't. We seem to have forgotten that a realistic performance number, with a thorough accounting for the gap between expectations and actual results, is a great reality check. Discomfort is a fabulous motivation to change and improve. Instead, what we have is institutionalized complacency and mediocrity based on fear.

Managers are afraid of the emotion involved when they give negative feedback. They are worried about your reaction, and so they sugar-coat the message or inflate their ratings. This has corrupted the system by changing its goals. Performance reviews are supposed to spur you on to turn your talent to great productivity and even better results, not just raise your morale or reassure and appease you.

You play your role in this corruption. Your inability to receive feedback with equanimity and your anxiety about accounting for your results leads you to blame others, or your circumstances, instead of taking responsibility. Guilt and emotional blackmail ensue when you fear your number may drop. You resist any change in your rating from year to year. You may resort to having a conversation about what your organization needs to give you in order to get the gift of your work.

Performance numbers have become ego numbers—a source of frustration and disappointment for most people. We tend to inflate not only our own performance but the performance of those around us. We want to feel we are giving our best. It's hard for your manager to be honest with you and hard for you to be honest with yourself. It's easy to look back over the previous year and overstate your accomplishments, especially when a promotion or a raise is at stake. But if you don't take account of your shortfalls and missed opportunities, you won't get the chance to learn from them.

Few people walk out of a performance review feeling thrilled about their feedback or clear on what they need to do to succeed. The most typical outcome is that your employer feels as though you are neither grateful enough for the inflated score nor committed enough to the organization, and that you're more focused on what you want to get than what you can give. And, even with an inflated score, you end up feeling undervalued, misunderstood, and under-rewarded for your hard work. Too often performance reviews become a source of confusion when you are told you are doing well at the same time the company is struggling. Or worse (as is happening today), the organization begins to align and recalibrate its performance ratings with its results, your numbers get real, and you are devastated to find that they were inflated in the first place. You get the false impression that the company's results have nothing to do with you—that the economy, poor leadership, your colleagues' lack of skill, or some other cause is to blame, and you as an employee are an innocent victim. After all, if you are the one working hard, as evidenced by your outstanding performance ratings, it must be other things, or people, effacing the success of the company.

While being let off the hook might feel okay, not being recognized for your contribution is a hollow experience. Feeling that your work has little real impact on the bottom line decreases your happiness, increases fear, and breeds resentment as reality continues to provide you with evidence you've been lied to. Many of you are playing defense, trying to establish minimal standards for which you can be rated as "meets expectations," focusing on what you have already given rather than what the organization needs to be competitive and how you can deliver it in the future.

How You Can Rise Above the Confusion

Regardless of what is wrong with reviews today, the bottom line is that company results are always a measurement of the talent inside, of the employees' ability to produce the desired results in their current circumstances. Your results are your fault and your responsibility. The old way was when you had a job deliverable, you delivered it, and

25

every year you got a raise. Those days are over. Meeting performance expectations is now the price of keeping your job. Performance is just one variable in the New Value Equation. By itself, it isn't enough to guarantee you anything extra—recognition, benefits, or job security. This is not an easy adjustment for many of us to make. But it is something you should acknowledge and embrace, because it means you have the potential to make a difference and be rewarded commensurate with your contribution.

To be valued, you must move beyond simply performing against the old standards. Your lack of raises can't be blamed on the economy. In the same day, from the same short budget, I have given one employee a 12 percent raise and said "No" to another. The successful employee was always working diligently to find ways to add more value. Willingness and focus will win rewards over time, every time.

The unsuccessful employee asked for a raise based on his increased living expenses. Compensation should be based on the value you add—not the needs you have. His threats to leave the company, while convincing, let me know I'd be better off freeing up those compensation dollars to reward others for the kind of performance I wanted to see. Increasingly, these are the kinds of decisions that make sense. That's why simply meeting expectations is not enough if you want to get ahead. At times when there isn't enough to go around, it becomes all the more important to be a low-drama, high-value player.

If you've always been a top performer, good for you—and, unfortunately, that's yesterday's news. Just to maintain its place in the market, your organization needs to provide greater value each year. It follows that your piece of those deliverables would also increase. What it takes this year to get a good rating should be greater than what it took last year. Yet many of you argue that if you are the same hardworking person as last year, this year you should garner the same rating—not understanding that effort doesn't always translate to value, and that the ante is raised from the outside each year.

When employees are asked to do more or different things, they sometimes react as if it isn't fair. In reality, goals must be raised every year to meet the ever growing challenges of business, increasing expectations of customers, and greater competition in the market-place. In Part Two, I show you how to rise to that challenge.

First, you need to look at your performance in a new way—as the price of admission to the game, one of several factors that determine where you stand. You have to do more than show up for work and be technically skilled, hardworking, and loyal. In order to get a true reflection of your total value to the organization and a reality check on what to fix in your performance to decrease your stress and increase your impact and happiness, it is vital that you rid yourself of defense and avoid the temptation to inflate your number out of ego.

I'm going to show you how to give yourself a true rating, from 1 to 5, based on rigorous criteria. Read the following descriptions and see where you best fit. To truly qualify for a rating, you must meet all the criteria in the category—not just most of the criteria. Base your rating on your actions—not your intentions. The outcomes of your work are what count, not just effort or how hard you perceive that you work. This is your private performance number that is going to show you what you need to work on to gain all the benefits I promised in the Introduction, so don't cheat yourself. The truth will be eye opening, and your first step toward true happiness and meaning at work.

Now, let's evaluate your current performance.

27

How to Rate Your Current Performance

Consider the following questions honestly, and rate yourself from 1 (lowest, not true) to 5 (highest, very true). *Base your ratings on your actions, not your intentions.*

I am on track to deliver on every goal outlined for me by my boss this year.

1. I am consistent in my attendance, my work, and my results.
2. I improve each year, as a matter of course, to keep up with changing expectations—without expecting more in return.
3. I am moving forward with purpose and not still taking credit for the accomplishments of years past.
4. The people I spend the most time with at work are top performers.
5. I have recently added to my job description on my own initiative.
6. I set goals for myself beyond the goals my supervisor sets.
7. I regularly ask for feedback on my performance from my boss and my peers.
8. My performance compares favorably with that of my peers, both in my company and in my industry.
9. I collaborate well with others and have good professional relationships.

Now, take the number of total points and divide by 10. That is your number for Current Performance. This can be a tough reality check if you have not been evaluated according to tough criteria like these in the past.

Now, let's examine further your Current Performance number as it pertains to the Value Equation (Your Value = Current Performance + Future Potential − 3 × Emotional Expensiveness).

Based on the assessment above, you fall somewhere on a continuum from 1 to 5, where

1 = Not meeting expectations
2 = Sometimes meeting expectations
3 = Fully meeting expectations
4 = Exceeding expectations
5 = Far exceeding expectations

Let's start with what it means to be a 1, not meeting expectations:

- You are not meeting any of the goals outlined by your boss for your performance this year.
- You are currently being tracked for an area of underperformance in your job.
- You have been told by your supervisor that you do not meet expectations.
- Your colleagues consider you unreliable.

Here is what it means to be a 2, barely meeting expectations:

- You are meeting some, not all, of the goals outlined by your boss for your work this year.
- You are inconsistent in your attendance, the quality of your work, and your results.
- You need frequent encouragement or monitoring in order to stay on task.
- You have occasional conflicts with your coworkers that require intervention by your supervisor.
- Your performance depends on what kind of day you're having and what is going on in your personal life at any given time.

Before we move on to the higher ratings, know that if you have scored a 1 or a 2 you are in a risky position and need to be willing to commit to a quick action plan to raise your number. The rest of this chapter—and the book—will help you do that. So don't despair, and keep reading.

Here is what it takes to be a 3, to meet expectations:

- You are currently delivering on or on track to meet every goal outlined by your boss for your work this year.
- You are fully meeting the expectations of your boss, your colleagues, and your customers.
- You are consistent in your attendance, your work, your results.
- You improve each year as a matter of course to keep up with changing times.
- You are open to feedback and seek out regular feedback from your supervisor and your colleagues.
- You work independently and need little assistance from others to conduct your core accountabilities—your daily responsibilities in your work.
- You strive to improve your performance on a regular basis.
- You are reliable, timely, and efficient.
- You are collaborative and a team player.
- You communicate well with others of all generations and backgrounds.
- You recognize, participate in, and support changing work requirements.

Having read this description, can you honestly say that you deserve a rating of 3? Only about 60 percent of people truly will. How far off are you?

For those of you who scored above a 3, let's move on. Here is a description of what it takes to be a 4, to exceed expectations:

- You are clearly considered by your boss and your colleagues to be an exceptional performer.
- You consistently exceed and surpass the communicated expectations of your job.
- Your outcomes and solutions are routinely excellent and seldom matched by others.
- You proactively identify needs and proactively generate solutions.
- Your achievements and contributions are obvious to your boss and coworkers.
- You contribute to the organization well above your job requirements.
- You are a role model for others.
- Others seek you out for assistance.
- You regularly make significant contributions to your area and organization's success well beyond your work assignments through your unique application of knowledge.

A few of you will qualify as a 4—remember, you have nothing to gain by over-rating yourself. Even fewer will qualify year after year. Be completely honest—only you need to know what your number is.

With a warning that hardly anyone is truly a 5, and even fewer maintain that level year after year, read on for a description of the highest level of performance, which far exceeds expectations:

- Your performance is truly exceptional.
- You consistently far exceed the expectations of your position.

31

- You consistently far exceed your goals.
- You have recent (that is, in this performance year) big wins that have contributed to the organization's success.
- You are a model of excellence in your behaviors of collaboration and communication as well as in your deliverables.
- You have a great deal of potential and are ready for advancement.
- You are actively teaching and mentoring others, sharing your knowledge, and contributing to others' improvement and success.
- You are one of the best the organization has ever seen.
- You are known in your profession and industry as a "go-to" person.
- You are responsible for breakthrough solutions or game-changing ideas that have added significant value to your organization.

Got Your Number? Now Raise It!

Now that you know your number, if it is anything under a 3, focus immediately on making changes that will improve your performance. Even if your boss has been inflating your rating and doesn't yet see the gap, you now know it is there, and you owe it to yourself to correct it before someone does it for you. The day of reckoning is coming, as organizations work to close the gap between individual performance ratings and the outcomes they are experiencing. So your performance score needs to be solid and sustainable.

If you scored a 3, know that you won't be able to ride on that score for long unless you are consistently working to keep up, improving your skills and knowledge to be able to perform far into the future. I talk more about that in the next chapter.

Even if you feel your score is high enough, there is always something you can be doing to shore up your performance rating and ensure that it is sustainable, no matter what numerical right-sizing goes on inside your organization or what new demands are put upon you from external forces in the marketplace.

Here are five questions to ask to help get, and keep, high, truthful, and sustainable performance numbers:

1. Who *are the top performers to emulate?* Find out who the top performers are in your company—those seen by the organization as curve-breakers. Don't resent them for breaking the curve and raising the bar. If you want what they have, go do what they did. Study them! Ask them to mentor you. In fact, why just seek the high performers out when in need? Hang with them whenever and however you can. You are the average of the five people you spend the most time with, so choose wisely.

2. What *are your goals?* Get clear on the expectations of your position. Revisit your job description, which, contrary to popular belief, is not there as a checklist to prove you are meeting expectations. Your job description represents the bare minimum expectations for your position—not what you need to do to succeed, but what you need to do *not to fail*. Elaborate on this foundation by writing an outline of the total scope of deliverables, accountabilities, and behaviors expected of you in your organization. Check your performance review, your team goals, your notes from team meetings and one-on-ones. Create a complete list of your commitments for this year. If you're not sure about any of the tasks on your list, ask for guidance, not just on what needs to be accomplished, but what it would take to exceed expectations. What does "great" look like? Ask for specific examples.

33

3. Where *do your goals fit into the big picture?* Now that you have clarity on your individual goals and role, get your organization's strategic plan and study it. Don't wait to be spoon-fed this important information. Make sure you understand your organization's goals, challenges, industry, environment, and how your goals fit in. Go deeper and understand why these strategies were adopted and created. What is the SWOT analysis of the company—what are its Strengths, Weaknesses, Opportunities, and Threats? How can you help strengthen the company by addressing those weaknesses in your own role and within your team? What are you doing right now to take full advantage of opportunities the organization has identified and to mitigate the threats and risks it faces? Get a very clear line of sight between what you do each day and how it fits in to the big picture, and deliver accordingly.

4. Why *keep your eyes on the prize?* Most people only look at their goals twice a year—when they create them and when they are about to be measured on them. Set yourself apart by reviewing yours often. Don't put your review and goals away in a file in your desk or on your computer, and for heaven's sake don't leave them with your boss for safe-keeping. Out of sight and out of mind, trust me. Having a visual reminder, whether it's a Post-it note next to your computer or a regular electronic alert to check in with yourself, will ensure your actions are consciously focused on your goals. Leave nothing to chance or surprise during your yearly review. You should know, at all times, exactly where you stand in relation to your deliverables. Check in with yourself regularly and ask, "Am I am on track and completing the tasks I committed to?" and the more important question, "Is my work creating the outcome and impact desired?" If your work is not adding the value to the organization that you mapped out in Steps 2 and 3, adjust! Check in with your boss and recalibrate early and often to

ensure that your effort is delivering results—and the desired results. Remember your rating isn't a rating of your effort, how hard you worked or how committed you were. It rates your outcomes.

5. How *will you reach your goals?* Make a plan for how to consistently exceed your daily accountabilities. Take each goal and map out your path to success. What exactly has to happen by when, and to what standard? Don't leave your success to a strategy of hope—track it. That which gets measured, gets accomplished. Last, be consistent. Lack of consistency is one of the biggest reasons that your rating can suffer. Anyone can deliver on a perfect day, or through heroics over a short period of time, but true value and trustworthiness is the result of consistent attendance, great attitude, and results with no surprises or let-downs. If you feel you are skilled and capable, but not getting the rating you want, work on consistency. Get into some of the good habits outlined in this book and those you observe in your industry's top performers.

The work you do to raise your performance number and create a plan of action for yourself is not just an investment in your future—it's a test of whether or not you are clear on expectations and competent in your position. Many people continue to go back to their bosses for "clarity" on these, in an attempt to not have to face the true reality: that they are not yet fully competent in the skills, knowledge, and abilities their jobs require. If you feel you are meeting expectations, but struggle with knowing how to deliver at a higher level, that is a problem we address in the next chapter.

Did you notice the difference between the ratings for "meets" and "exceeds" expectations? It's all about the extras. Don't just do what's necessary—go above and beyond what is asked of you. Fix your performance now, and you will be prepared and even immune to any upcoming changes in these ratings that are so closely tied to your compensation. This is the mandatory first step that will take one huge source of stress off the table for you. Then you can focus on the rest of your equation and on moving from surviving to thriving; from dreading work to enjoying work. I want you to start proactively looking for your next opportunity to improve the way you work and get busy developing yourself. Chapter Two, on Future Potential, will show you how.

2

Your Future Potential

Growth in any company requires employees and leaders to challenge themselves to grow and call one another up to greatness. Yet Future Potential is something that almost no one is measuring. We spend most of our time measuring what we did in the past and trying to survive the present. When I go out on speaking tours, people often tell me that their jobs have become too big. They are expected to produce more results with fewer resources: fewer people, smaller budgets, less time. If this is not true in your job today, it will almost certainly be true in the future. However, these arguments about performance, efforts to explain why performing to expectations is increasingly difficult in current circumstances, only distract us from developing our potential. You can—and should—be aiming higher than survival of the next round of layoffs. Instead of trying to protect yourself from changing circumstances and expectations on the horizon, you need to grow into them.

I give Performance and Future Potential equal weight in the Value Equation because your job will not remain static in description or expectations. When people tell me that their jobs are too big, what I hear is that they are not adapting in the ways that they need to, to keep pace with the new demands. Let's be clear: I'm on their side. And I'm on your side. You deserve to feel excited about your future, but your feeling about the future—whether excitement or dread—is directly correlated to your level of readiness and your vision for what's next. Great news: your Future Potential is totally within your control. In this chapter, I show you what Future Potential demands and how to calculate your current value for this factor in the New Value Equation. Then, I give you five tactics that will help you maximize it. Let's start with some counterintuitive advice: If you want to move toward a compelling vision for your future, you need to start from a place of pain. That may sound counterintuitive, because often pain just makes us want to quit. I show you how pain can lead to great outcomes in the future.

When You Want to Quit

In *Reality-Based Leadership*, I introduced leaders to the shocking statistic that 68 percent of their workforce quits every day—in their heads. They keep coming to work and collecting a paycheck, but in their hearts and minds, they have checked out. Most people on the other side of the desk are not at all surprised to hear this statistic, because you live it. You overhear the conversations in the elevator and the lunch room that your boss doesn't. I call that "the meeting after the meeting," where everyone gets together to talk about how messed up things are and how "they" don't understand what "we" do and they need to (fill in the blank) if they want us to (fill in the blank). While you get the benefit of the doubt—you are probably one of the 32 percent who refuse to participate in these mental walk-outs—there is no one among us who can say we haven't sometimes quit at least part of our jobs: the parts we failed to prepare for or the parts we don't like. What usually happens when we are confronted with a change or a challenge in our jobs is a predictable pattern of surprise, panic, and blame.

Even my most-loved jobs have had elements I disliked or was unprepared for. In my current job, many times it's the constant air travel. I can't say I love to fly multiple times a week, so I often approach my flights ill prepared, taking the final flight out of town so I can savor every last moment at home with my kids. I arrive at the airport at the last minute, leaving myself little flexibility for when things change, as they inevitably do. I have essentially quit part of my job—checking my reservations and status, planning, and taking earlier flights to accommodate changing schedules. After I have stepped down, rather than stepped up, to my own responsibilities, I find it so easy to slip into the feigned surprise: "Wow, I didn't see that coming"; through to the panic: "Will I miss my connection?"; and finally blame: of the airlines, the travel planner, the weather, and even my loved ones for insisting on living in a winter climate. You see where this is going? Eventually, whether I like my sudden change of plans or not, I'm going to have to make the best of it. Why not start there and save myself some time? Is this pattern sounding familiar to you?

When surprise, panic, and blame fail to satisfy, we fantasize about retirement. We check our 401(k) portfolios, buy lottery tickets, and hope a rich relative we don't know will die and leave us a trust fund. But the truth is, people are horrible at quitting. We may be doing our jobs for more than a paycheck, and I certainly hope you have other reasons to come to work in the morning, but mortgages, car payments, and college loans continue to exist. They keep us all busy, but we aren't necessarily working. No, we're taking a spin in our BMWs—Bitching, Moaning, and Whining Wagons. That's when we tend to do the kind of "problem solving" that is about coming up with what everyone else needs to do to solve our problems. We get together and gas up one another's BMWs with more reasons, stories, and excuses for why we can't possibly deliver what has been asked of us. We step down instead of stepping up and then make up a story about why we had to. We make lists of what we would need in order to make it work: "I need a different boss, one who cares. I need no one to ask me for anything without notice. I need the rules to stop changing." We look for people to agree with us and keep us company in our outrage. In our hearts, we have quit. And we're not honest about it. Think about what that would sound like if you had to justify your every moment to your boss: "You paid me for three hours last Thursday when I was hating your guts and complaining behind your back about the new computer system and, karmically, I can't accept your money. So here's a check for $45...."

From Pain ... to Vision

The people winning today greet change with a simple "Good to know." They aren't shocked. It's just information to them. Instead of complaining about your job getting bigger, there not being enough staff, and your company's expectations changing, you need to get more efficient with your energy and step up to development opportunities as a matter of course. The more you look at it as a chance to grow, the better off you'll be. Your success must not depend on everything staying the same in your job or industry—that's a recipe for disaster. Get zealous about development. Just going to company-delivered training and keeping up with your field's continuing education requirements is not enough. You need to do more to stay relevant and competent. And the place to start is where it hurts the most. What is it you dread more than anything else? What wakes you up in the night with palpitations? Whatever it is, get to work on that first. Your anxiety or stress is caused by your inability to deliver given your current skills, abilities, methods, and capabilities, not by outrageous expectations. How do I know? Just take a look at the reality—others are delivering within the same constraints and with the same challenges both inside your organization and at your competitors. That proves it is possible, when you stop protecting the status quo and coming up with reasons why you shouldn't have to do something instead of focusing on how you can. Where are you spending your time and energy? Resisting or preparing?

Get clear on the source of your suffering. It's your lack of readiness, not the new requirements or circumstances. One way out of pain is to evolve quicker than the needs of your organization. Surrender early and use the energy you might otherwise waste on resistance to fuel your growth instead.

One of my clients, Ellen, was at her wit's end at work. She and her team work for a company that uses proprietary software to produce timely and accurate invoices for all kinds of businesses throughout North America. Her leaders wanted to expand the company's remit to take in the Asia/Pacific and European markets. The prospect exhausted them because they were only just managing to stay on top of the demand for their services in the United States. How would they maintain their level of service in the United States while taking on new markets with the same size team? Ellen was so stressed about it that she considering quitting. When she encountered my Reality-Based philosophy, she realized that

41

she needed to expand her own skill set before she could help expand the business abroad. She said, "Last year we had ten initiatives we were working on—things internally we had to accomplish. Those ten were brought down to eight during the year due to critical issues with customers, emergencies that we had to drop everything to resolve. I realized we were always 'reacting' in the moment and not anticipating—that's why we were never able to get ahead. We were just stabilizing—we weren't growing."

The bottom line of this story is that a request to take on more work seemed like a slap in the face—a denial of how busy this team was already. The team shared a common belief that they were already working at their highest potential, and when the request came in, they quickly colluded together to agree that it was unreasonable. But their stress wasn't caused by the new request; it was caused by their own lack of readiness, their over-reliance on heroics at the expense of implementing and staying accountable to good processes. Their need for development in these areas was exposed when they were asked to do more with the same resources. It was only by facing their pain and acknowledging their need for development that they were able to get out of pain and successfully deliver on the new expectations. Ellen and the rest of the team were up to the challenge: "We had to get in control of our processes—really document them and know them inside and out—before we could begin to anticipate what might happen next, and prepare in advance so we're not simply reacting all the time. This year our team is growing and expanding, even with fewer people than last year. Instead of adjusting our expectations down, we have found we can exceed our goals."

This was a job of catch-up spurred on by pressure from their organization, and although it was fraught with a bit of panic, in the end they stepped up and they've been reaping the benefits ever since.

Here are some other examples of what can happen when we believe that our pain is caused by our circumstances, when in fact it is just our circumstances exposing where we need to develop or adapt next:

- We get furious when things change and blame others for not making and keeping priorities clear, when in fact we need to develop flexibility.
- We panic when we are not given all the information and blame our bosses for letting us down, when in fact we need to develop our ability to deal with ambiguity.
- We blame marketing for not getting us the materials we needed for the big presentation, when in fact we need to develop project management skills to clearly lay out project plans and milestones for tracking.
- We blame our senior leadership team for not addressing our concerns, when in fact we need to develop courage, to ask the questions that are on our minds.

If you regularly bench-press 25 pounds and someone suddenly asks you to lift 75, you can't do it and may even go on to argue it isn't physically possibly for someone your age. But when you can lift 25 pounds easily, you can move up to 30, then 35, then 40. By the time expectations change, 75 may seem like a stretch goal, but not an impossibility. You've anticipated the change and prepared for it. You may even be excited. You certainly won't be afraid to try.

If you do not continually adapt to new circumstances and begin to anticipate change in advance, you will become overwhelmed. It may not happen immediately; it may even seem like the easier option. But over time, it will really hurt your understanding and your long-term prospects. Imagine you're reading a book and you come across a word you've never seen before. You have two choices: to pause and look it up, or to keep reading and hope for the best. The second strategy is easier in the short term—it doesn't require any action on your part. But as you continue to read, if you fail to guess the word's meaning, your misunderstanding could affect your comprehension of the sentence or paragraph. There's no shame in not knowing everything, whether it's a matter of vocabulary or a new system at work. The shame comes when you don't take the opportunity to learn.

Most people waste energy on complaints and self-limitation when they could be anticipating the next challenge and moving toward it with alacrity. Your mind-set has everything to do with your success. We tend to believe our pain is coming from increased expectations and demands and rarely consider that it might actually be coming from our response to those demands, our lack of growth and readiness, and our fear of failure. When people say they are overwhelmed, they often say that it's because they don't have enough time to do what they need or want. The reality is that everyone has the same amount of time in a day. Some people just use their time more effectively than others. Someone with a victim mind-set says, "I don't have enough time," whereas an accountable person says, "I'm not using my time wisely," and works to develop better prioritization skills. No one can run the risk of falling behind. If your development flat-lines and your industry moves on, you become irrelevant very quickly and leave yourself with only the option of resisting change rather than jumping on board.

When I first got promoted in health care, I was floored by the number of meetings I was required to attend. I quickly came to believe that I simply did not have enough time to attend all the meetings and run my department and coach my people. Even at the meetings, my coworkers and I colluded and agreed that the problem with our jobs was that we had too many meetings and too little time allotted to get it all done. And then I had a breakthrough insight. Was it really that I didn't have enough time (the resource

I felt I was lacking)? Or was it something else? Each of us had resigned ourselves to the fact that we all needed to be present for every meeting, in case someone tried to make a decision without considering our department. Could the problem be that we as a team didn't have enough trust among us? We weren't able to lessen the number of meetings in the short term or to come up with more time in a day, but I realized that I could work on choosing to trust my colleagues and educating them on my area so that they could represent my interests in meetings, and vice versa. We could take turns. When one of us attended, she represented all of us and could always "phone a friend" during the meeting if in need of an answer.

By developing our ability to trust each other and to prep each other for meetings, we cut our mandatory meetings down by 75 percent. What I thought was the source of my pain—too many meetings and not enough time—wasn't. Seeing my circumstances differently and working to develop myself in competencies I was lacking turned out to be the solution (but only always). That is why potential is so incredibly important. It is entirely possible to grow and develop yourself out of any pain, and when you are growing and developing as a matter of course, you push for change so you can use all those new skills and avoid getting bored.

Now, let's evaluate your Future Potential.

How to Rate Your Future Potential

Consider the following questions honestly, and rate yourself from 1 (lowest, not true) to 5 (highest, very true). Base your ratings on your actions, not your intentions.

1. I make an effort to learn as much as I can about changes that will affect me.

2. If I want something, I work hard to get it.
3. When something good happens to me, I feel it is because I've earned it.
4. Failure is a great teacher, and I work to extract its lessons.
5. I am an early adopter of new technology that can help me do my job better.
6. A person can change his personality and behavior patterns.
7. I work to change or improve regardless of whether my boss has identified a need for development.
8. For the issues that have come up in the past three months, I can identify specific things I could have done differently to change the outcome.
9. I am involved in mentoring others.
10. I have participated in a development experience that was not funded or arranged by my organization in the past year.

Now, take the number of total points and divide by 10. That is your current number for Future Potential. Does it seem fair to you? If you're thinking you're overrating or underrating yourself, rest assured that the marketplace will let you know when you have it right.

The following descriptions outline what it means to be at each level. Remember that to qualify for a rating, you must meet all of its criteria, not just some.

Now, let's examine further your Future Potential number as it pertains to the Value Equation (Your Value = Current Performance + Future Potential − 3 × Emotional Expensiveness). Based on the assessment above, you fall somewhere on a continuum from 1 to 5 where

1 = Being quickly outdated
2 = Complacent, not trying hard enough

3 = Keeping up with expectations
4 = Exceeding expectations
5 = Leading the pack

Let's start with what it means to be a 1—among those who are being quickly outdated:

- You pine for the simpler times you experienced in the past.
- You are often stressed at work and feel you can't keep up.
- You are not tech savvy and avoid an online presence.
- You resist further education by not signing up for and attending training sessions set up by your company.
- You do not belong to any industry networking groups.

Here is what it means to be a 2, who is complacent and not trying hard enough:

- You like to be sure that you will use what you learn before you go to the trouble of learning it.
- You will make improvements to how you work once someone else identifies a development need.
- You feel in conflict—either direct or indirect—with coworkers from generations other than your own.
- You often feel your job is too big.
- If all of your coworkers are in a social media group, you'll go ahead and join, too.

Here is what it takes to be a 3, to keep up with expectations:

- You learn new skills and gain new competencies as required for your job.

- You will adopt new technology once others in your industry recommend it to you or require it from you.
- You participate in development experiences when your company funds and arranges them.
- You often feel you are in survival mode, always racing to integrate new technologies or expectations before a deadline, but you meet the deadline.
- You follow the trends in your industry.

Here is what it means to be a 4, exceeding expectations:

- You seek out new challenges.
- You are fluent in a variety of social media.
- You are a vigorous learner and have a long list of activities and books you're reading at any given time.
- You are an early adopter of technology that may help you do your job better.
- You work to extract the lessons from your failures and disappointments.

Here is what it means to be a 5, to lead the pack:

- You are always trying to improve how you work, regardless of whether your boss identifies a need.
- You will try anything on for size—whether it's a new technology or a new role.
- You have a large and active social network.
- You surround yourself with diverse people, generations, and thoughts.
- Change doesn't scare you because you're confident you can figure it out—or else someone in your huge network will help you.

- You often participate in development experiences that your company does not fund or arrange.
- You belong to a trendsetting group or are considered a trendsetter in your industry.
- You're seen as someone with succession or leadership potential.
- You share information freely so others won't be left behind.
- You have a mentor, and you are a mentor.

Having read this description, can you honestly say you deserve a rating of 5? Not many people do. Most will fall below this standard.

Got Your Number? Now Raise It!

If you are rating yourself a 3 or lower, there is a good chance that the only people worried about your development are in the Human Resources Department. That is a high-risk strategy for your Future Potential. It's probable that your focus on wishing for different circumstances is robbing you of your development in the very areas that you need to improve to be happy and successful. It's time to put real effort into your Future Potential by figuring out what you need to work on to stay relevant in the future and succeed in spite of your circumstances.

Five Tactics for Maximizing Your Future Potential

Following are five tactics for improving your future potential. My advice to you is to find the one that causes you the most anxiety or resistance—and start there. The antidote to worry is to take the first step toward a goal. Then the second. In order to get to vision, you have to move through pain, but the results will be worth it.

Tactic #1: Get Reflective

If you have scored a 3 or lower for Future Potential, look back at what it would take to score a 5. Make a list of where you're falling short. How do you compare to people applying for similar jobs to your own right now? Would you be the top candidate if you were interviewing for your job? What have you skimped on, what do you fear, where have you fallen behind? You can't fix what you don't know—or won't admit—is broken. Get a coach or find a mentor in your industry. Now is the time to invest in yourself and your future.

If you are lucky enough to have a mentor or receive coaching from someone at work, show your willingness and enthusiasm. Bring them meaningful evidence of your commitment and what you have learned. Coaching that doesn't lead to action is free therapy. It's not just "See you next week." It's "With your help, I fixed this problem. What do I need to work on next?" Use your coach to improve yourself, not to try to improve your workplace. The idea is not to change your reality—it's to get you capable of delivering in any reality.

Don't be afraid to ask anyone for advice. Your manager is only one of many good sources of ideas for growth. In Part Two, I go into depth on the best ways to ask for, and accept, feedback. A great concept that I learned from Marshall Goldsmith is Feedforward.[1] Unlike feedback, which is focused on learning from your past actions, Feedforward is focused on what you will do in the future. You set a goal for yourself and then go ask as many people as you can find who have achieved that goal for two suggestions on what you can do to achieve it. These conversations can be quick and to the point and need not begin and end with people you know well or with whom you work. The key is to take in all suggestions without criticism and then follow up with a review of the suggestions and pick a few that you believe would work for you. This is an easy way to create a plan for your development. When I decided to write a book, I did the Feedforward exercise, asking anyone I could think of who makes a living as a writer, and they were very generous with tips to help me get started and overcome common obstacles, such as finding time to write, facing the blank page, structuring my thoughts, finding an agent, and getting a publisher.

Tactic #2: Get Beyond the Baseline

What are you doing with the opportunities you have? A year in your job, no matter what level in the hierarchy, likely affords you several opportunities to take a class, get extra training, or improve your credentials in the form of optional computer skills classes or mentor programs. Smart organizations assess who takes advantage of these opportunities. If you are offered extra training by your company, consider it part of your education—show willingness and really put that opportunity to use. Before any course, set yourself a goal for what you intend to take away from it—the way you intend to change your behavior. Ask yourself, "Have I used the tools I've been given to do my job? Or am I just asking for more tools?"

Even as you take advantage of this extra training, know that it only represents a baseline, the minimum requirement to keep your head above water. That isn't enough. Many people are required to attain a minimum number of continuing education credits per year in order to maintain their licenses or professional status. And they mostly do just that—the minimum. If you only do what is required by your employer or a professional licensing organization, you will never reach the top of your profession. If you don't distinguish yourself from the average, you can't expect to get above-average results or rewards. If you are not seeking out your own opportunities, you are not maximizing your Future Potential. To truly get ahead of the curve—to become and remain a curve-breaker who adds great value and avoids the pain of falling behind, you must get zealous about learning and growth.

Zealous learners do more than take classes. Classes can be great if you commit to using what you learn, but if you attend passively and change nothing in your daily life as a result, they are a waste of time. They are also "safe" in that they require nothing of you but attendance. According to research by Michael M. Lombardo and Robert W. Eichinger for the Center for Creative Leadership,[2] classes account for only about 10 percent of development. Their 70:20:10 model states that the majority of development—a whopping 70 percent—comes from on-the-job experiences, like joining project teams, accepting new assignments, in short, saying "Yes" to every opportunity that comes your way (and, I would add, making your own opportunities). The other 20 percent of our development comes from others, through feedback, mentoring, and coaching. So don't just wait for your employer to have a class and offer it up to you. Focus on your Future Potential by taking on new challenges and getting beyond the baseline.

Tactic #3: Get Challenged

Complacency is one of the biggest risks to your Future Potential. Your Future Potential depends on your learning agility and your passion for your own evolution. When was the last time you learned a new skill? Subscribed to a journal that was not required reading? Tried something new that you could fail at without fear?

Be the type of person who enjoys learning and exercises those muscles often. If you say you're bored—what you are saying to me is you have become boring. Get interested and evolve both inside and outside the workplace. You can't expect anyone else to work harder at your success than you do. Downtimes are perfect times to upgrade your skill set, volunteer for cross-training, widen your experience by accepting lateral moves within the company, and enhance your value by becoming more flexible—a great utility player who knows the industry and the business itself. Develop yourself with outside experiences such as volunteer work, board involvement, and continuing education. Be willing to take on additional responsibility, especially when it builds your capabilities and ultimately your résumé.

Offer to take on an extra project, especially if it relates to a skill you are working on or a development need you have identified for yourself. Your manager should be able to count on you to make him or her look good. That said, get your accomplishments in front of more people than your direct manager at every opportunity. When it comes to potential, managers can have incredible blind spots. If someone new joins their department, and they teach them everything they know, the risk is that they will continue seeing their mentee as the "new kid" long after this is an accurate reflection of the person's status and skill. It may not be fair, but it is common. The right kinds of interactions with leadership are development opportunities that you should court—not shy away from.

Tactic #4: Get Connected

Sometimes it's necessary to go through a few months of adjustment and growing pains just to stay current. It is no longer avoidable. New technology, in particular, gets integrated without much discussion these days. Everyone is going through the same thing. You have a choice to lean forward into it and bond with your colleagues over a shared challenge, or resist. Resistance takes longer. It's emotionally draining. It holds you back in your career and can make you less employable on a skills level and in terms of your attitude. Where is the upside, for you or for your company?

If you were in the workplace fifteen years ago, you'll remember when computers with Internet connections became standard equipment in most companies. At first, chaos reigned as people figured out how these new toys worked and learned the new etiquette surrounding them. ("Reply all"? Verboten. Chain letters? Please no. Being able to exchange a quick message with a friend without having to take a personal phone call? Win.)

At the time, it seemed that every company had its share of holdouts. In those early years, especially if you were a chief executive office or a VIP with an assistant, you could get away with insisting that he or she print each e-mail out and type your dictated response. Fifteen years later, try hiring a personal assistant for one of these dinosaurs. It's not acceptable anymore—BlackBerries and iPhones put a stop to that. Now, if you haven't responded to an e-mail within a day, people assume you're not interested. A world of business opportunities will pass you by while you're busy printing and filing all those e-mails.

Put tech savvy on project status. Don't just learn your company's new system—it's bound to change soon. Instead, learn how to learn systems. Use a Mac and a PC. Use a variety of types of phones so you stay flexible. Join LinkedIn, Twitter, Facebook, and other social networks—but keep your image pristine. And if you don't know how, learn to type, for heaven's sake.

Improving our future potential requires not only tech savvy (or a willingness to attain it) but an important related element: how much you're interacting with the world of pop culture. When was the last time you downloaded a new app? Do you know what Spotify is? If you are still trying to figure out how to upload a photo to your

Facebook timeline, that's a bad sign. If you have no idea who Lady Gaga or Lil' Wayne are, if you've never heard of the iPhone app that allows you to instantly identify songs, if you have never played Angry Birds . . . Be careful how you rated yourself earlier.

I thought I was in touch with current tech culture, but while hanging out in an airport bar, I got a reality check of my own. I had a layover and there was a playoff game on TV. There were several TVs in the bar, all tuned to Brazilian soccer. I asked the bartender if we could change the channel and she said it was against the bar's policy—that once a requested game had begun, another customer's request could not trump it and the game would be on for the duration. I was finding the policy a little ridiculous, given that I was the only person in the bar and whoever had requested the game was long gone, perhaps on a flight to Brazil! I was frustrated, feeling I had no impact on the situation, contemplating having to move all my stuff to another venue. Meanwhile, a young guy came into the bar and sat down next to me. He took one look at the TV and said, "Hey, where's the playoffs?" I told him what was going on and instead of leaving he said, "Hey—that's an iPhone, right?" I handed him my iPhone and within about a minute he had downloaded an app for a universal remote, and we were watching the playoffs. I bought him a beer and for the next hour, we watched the game. But that's not the best part. I have a universal remote control on my iPhone, which means I basically rule the airport now. I get to watch whatever I want! While that ended in a great victory for me, I must say that when it comes to technology and keeping up, I am humbled on a daily basis by what I have yet to learn and utilize. If you follow sports, you quickly absorb the lesson that nothing is sacred—no limit or record is permanent. Great athletes keep surpassing themselves and each other. That attitude keeps everyone performing at their personal best.

Tactic #5: Get Multigenerational

At this point in time, three generations coexist in the workplace, and each has its strengths and weaknesses. Get clear on what your generation brings to the table and what you need to learn from the other two.

Those of you nearing retirement have experience to offer. Pass on your trade secrets, the knowledge and unique skills you have perfected over the years. Document what's in your head so others can benefit. Stop judging the younger generations and teach them instead, without righteousness or shaming. Release yourself from the need to see others "pay their dues"—trust me, they are and they will. Your helping them won't change that, but if you do choose to help instead of editorializing on what's wrong with them, they'll remind you of your idealistic years and give you plenty in return. From them, you'll rediscover the pleasure of entertaining the impossible, shaking things up a bit, and connecting with the world from a sense of possibility.

If you look back to your early years in your profession, they likely involved a leap of faith. Chances are it was a mentor or a coworker who inspired you to buy in and make a career out of your job. If you have been in your profession for a while, you have the opportunity to share your experience, sense of purpose, and inspiration with someone just starting out. You might even find the inspiration flows both ways. You can lend them some of your credibility you have earned over the years by endorsing them and their ideas. You can help them identify flaws in their logic in a positive way and help them to improve their ideas to address your concerns.

Refuse to retire while you are still working. If you stop evolving now, you are headed for a tough ending to a great career. The runway is just too short—the change is coming too fast. You can't wait out the time. Besides, why stop developing now? Think of your life after retirement. I doubt you are planning to just do time, hang out, and wait till the end. What you learn today will help determine the quality of life you have tomorrow and in the days to come.

There is a narrative about the youngest generation in the workplace that they are hard to work with, that they have a sense of entitlement, that they are takers who want everything handed to them on a silver platter. When I make comments like this, my son often asks, "Well, who raised us?" Besides, it is simply not true. They are no different from any previous generation to arrive, fresh from college with its clear reward system and their parents, who may have overpraised them just a little. How is that different from the way you were when you started out? We all entered the workforce over-rewarded and under-coached. If you can't have a conversation with anyone younger than you, how can you expect to stay relevant and employable into the future?

My advice to those of you mid-career is to be bridge builders. You raised the younger generation, and you were raised by the older generation. You have great translation skills to offer, so step up and adapt. Don't be afraid to give feedback to both generations. Adopt the newest members of the workforce. Let them teach you, in particular, when it comes to technology. Quit dabbling and jump in with both feet. Ask questions, but don't let them do it for you because you need equal fluency to ensure your future employability and success. Besides, it's fun. This generation will remind you that work can include play, and many of you need reminding. In return, you can coach the younger generation on behaviors and standards they need to maintain in order to get where you are. People with great Future Potential aren't just learning continually—they also teach. Hoarding information will not safeguard your position—quite the opposite. Instead, become known for bringing people with you, whether they are on your level or below. We all have to start somewhere. Who inspired you?

The one thing that is fair to say about the new generation in the workplace is that they are really intolerant of slow, inefficient ways of doing things. So if they know of a technology that will help them do something better, faster, cheaper—they will. Don't be afraid to ask them to teach it to you. And whatever you do, don't play the role of the curmudgeon. "In my day . . ." blocks your future potential and brands you an out-of-touch Luddite. Those kids might just be smarter than you in some ways, so give them a chance.

To the new generation: we love that you come with great new skill sets and shortcuts made possible by your fluency in technology and creative new ways of approaching work. Share your optimism and your exuberance for finding new and better ways, but don't diss the old ways. They worked until you came. Offer help, but don't be overbearing about it. Be careful what you think you know for sure. Get adopted quickly by mentors who will fill in the gaps in your knowledge about the history and complexity of your organization. And whatever you do, don't skimp on the basics like attendance and consistency. Regardless of the high-level contributions you make in other aspects of your job, without building this foundation, you won't get the credibility that allows others to trust you with bigger and better projects.

Your parents may have neglected to teach you some things in their desire to protect you and develop your self-esteem. In the real world, everyone doesn't get a trophy. There are winners and losers, and it is vital that you hold up your end of the bargain. You have a lot to offer, but you need development on the behaviors that will make you successful in the business world. For better or worse, the workplace will be your finishing school, so do not underestimate what you need to learn and keep learning. Those folks who seem to you today to be irrelevant and out of date were once high-performing, capable young professionals who didn't get mentors to show them the way. Without great coaching and feedback, they slowly became righteous and irrelevant. They were the same people who were quickly replaced by the next generation. You are not immune to the same phenomenon. Don't be the next group of employees to decide they are right and everyone else is wrong. Don't see others as the barrier to your success, but as the avenue to your success. Pay attention to what they tell you—combine the great new things your generation brings with a great knowledge of what works at work, and you will go far.

If all of this sounds like a lot of work, like more "to do's" on your already full list, don't look at it that way. You won't really be doing more—just expending your existing energy in a different way. When you get willing and step up to your current expectations and prepare for the future, each investment in learning ensures that your work will get easier, not harder, and that it will become more exciting and energizing. We are at our best when we are challenged. Growth and movement beget more growth and movement. Overcoming inertia, having to stop and start all the time, especially on a steep development curve, is what wears us out. Keep in continuous forward motion and your energy will be continually fed, not wasted.

If you want to raise your number, you can't just show up and collect your paycheck—you have to produce results today and well into the future. If you look at how many people out there are doing the least they can get away with, that gives you some idea of how easy it will be to pass them by for promotions and jobs. I think of it like this: If you and some other people were trying to outrun a hungry tiger, you would not actually have to be faster than the tiger. You would just have to be faster than at least one of the other people trying to escape.

Development is no longer in the hands of the organization or the leader. It's back in your hands, where it belongs. Time to own it for yourself through experience, exposure, networks, curiosity, risk taking, evolving, pursuing, questioning—in short, being as willing, open minded, and open hearted as you can.

Now you have determined your Current Performance and Future Potential numbers. You may be wondering why performance plus potential don't add up to value. I wish it were that simple. If it weren't for the last factor in the value equation, Emotional Expensiveness, I wouldn't have had to write a book at all. But when you look at employee performance and potential, it isn't the whole picture. Even a slow leak can sink a ship, and many employees are unwittingly doing just that. Emotional Expensiveness is the third factor in the Value Equation. Paradoxically, it is the most important in determining your value, because while Performance and Potential are what you add to the bottom line, Emotional Expensiveness is what you take away.

3

Your Emotional Expensiveness

U ntil recently, Emotional Expensiveness has been the invisible affliction in the workplace. Everyone has had the experience of working with someone who, while performing his or her job unimpeachably, exacts a high cost for that performance. Almost all of you are familiar with the concept of "high" versus "low" maintenance when it comes to relationships and would be capable of categorizing your friends and family according to this rubric—who's bringing drama, who's not; who, in aggregate, is more of a "taker" than a "giver." For some of us, it's as simple as the feeling we get when someone's number comes up on our phone screens—whether we take the call immediately, without hesitation, or roll our eyes and let it go to voicemail. Emotional Expensiveness is something we can afford to be lighthearted about in our personal relationships (and, when it comes to family, we don't get to choose, so laughing may be our best option). But have you ever considered the impact of drama in your workplace? The following examples—one funny, one classic—will show you Emotional Expensiveness in action. Both stories are true.

An ad executive I worked with had the ultimate example of Emotional Expensiveness in one of his employees. This employee would throw toddler-like tantrums—everything but the breath-holding—when things did not go his way at work. Once he threw himself on the sofa in the lobby, kicking and screaming, disrupting everyone's day and giving them something to talk about for weeks to come. He was summarily fired. The executive told me, "We're in a service business and we're here to serve. We aren't going to be the kind of agency that tolerates diva behavior, no matter how talented you are."

Another example of Emotional Expensiveness is the righteous top performer. A lawyer I worked with was growing tired of pussyfooting around a senior paralegal at her office. Other partners in the firm feared losing her to the competition, but they acknowledged that she was difficult to work with. Her skill level was unmatched within her department, but she was whiny and passive aggressive, lording her seniority over the other paralegals, requiring the lawyers to cultivate her favor, and withholding her effort when she saw fit. Annual review time and bonus time were particularly fraught. No matter what she got, she was never happy. Eventually, the partners came to see that she was not as valuable as they thought she was. Her cost far outweighed her contribution, and she was a drag on the whole firm. My client stated, "You can't bill for hours you spend managing difficult people—and it is a significant investment of time." At the paralegal's next review, when she complained about her situation yet again, the firm did not capitulate to her demands. The lawyer reviewing her asked instead what she planned to do to become happier in her position and match her attitude to her skill level. She was taken aback and could see that their attitude toward her had changed. Her habitual behavior was not getting the results she sought. Within six weeks, the problem paralegal resigned, and the firm was able to hire another paralegal who, while not as experienced, was a better cultural fit and, in the new scheme of things, more valuable.

You may have known someone like this at your office and seen the costs of extreme Emotional Expensiveness firsthand. Employers have wised up and are less and less willing to deal with Emotionally Expensive people. They now understand the true cost and they prefer not to pay it when they could be working with the willing. A consultant friend was secretly gleeful when his boss—who had made loads of money for the firm over the previous decade while ensuring that all his underlings lived in a state of perpetual dread—was finally offloaded for just that reason. It turned out his bosses didn't much like him, either, and they knew people who could do his job cheaper, in all senses of the word.

For the moment, I want to put those extreme examples aside. Emotional Expensiveness is not the sole province of the tantruming ad exec, the self-righteous paralegal, or the nightmare boss. We are all guilty of it on some level, and I do not exclude myself. You may be Emotionally Expensive if . . .

- You are dramatic—drama requires a big investment, but the ROI is zero. In fact, it is negative.
- You come to work in a bad mood. Ever.
- You share a lot of personal information with coworkers, and the boundary between your public life and private life is very permeable.

63

- You complain a lot, or judge others.
- You have an entitled or a victim mind-set—about anything from the snacks in the vending machine to the brand of pens the company stocks.
- You tend to focus on what you need rather than what you have.
- You assume the worst motivations for others' behavior—especially when you are not in a position to know their true motives. "They did it on purpose," "They are trying to sabotage me," or "They aren't as dedicated as I am...." How would you know?
- You use your boss's open door as a place to vent about your job or coworkers.
- You wait for things to happen instead of making them happen.
- When things don't go as planned, you find excuses and blame others or your circumstances. "HR won't let us," "We were never told that," or "We didn't have enough staff."
- When you perform well, you want a medal for it.
- You play the martyr when asked to do something beyond your job description.
- You and your friends at work spend time complaining about the boss or gossiping about coworkers.
- You enjoy being proven right, even if your prediction was a negative one.
- You spend time looking for ways other people can improve your situation, or thinking that they should.

Being Emotionally Expensive saps your productivity as well as that of those around you. Emotional Expensiveness is why you were passed over for a promotion. Emotional Expensiveness is why meetings are fraught. Emotional Expensiveness is why you don't love coming to work every day like you did when you first started your job. Emotional Expensiveness is also what is draining and killing most organizations—not poor leadership, outsourcing, corporate policies, or government regulation.

Rating Emotional Expensiveness

I calculate Emotional Expense, like Performance and Potential, on a five-point continuum, but in this instance the higher the number, the worse the implications. Here's what I mean:

A 5 is the quintessential drama king or queen who sucks the air out of the room with high-maintenance demands. Or the martyr/victim who is passive aggressive, focused on what he lacks and looking for someone to blame when things go wrong. A 5 is someone whose car you dread to see in the parking lot. Depending on your own personality and your relationship with the 5, you will either avoid her when you see her in the hall, or you'll be thrilled to see her because your day is about to get "interesting." Fives, thankfully, are very rare.

You don't have to be the diva chief executive officer whose assistant is crying in the bathroom to cost more than you're worth—you could be a 4. A 4 could be someone who is professionally brilliant but has a tendency to eat her own young, treating newbies on the job with hostility and insisting that they learn things the hard way. For example, the kind of person who gives little feedback or challenge, except when given the opportunity to criticize or make a point in front of an audience. Or the kind of person who takes credit for others' work. Or the kind of person who throws coworkers under the bus to save his or her own reputation. Or the kind whose direct reports stagnate and quit instead of moving up through the organization and contributing their talent for years to come. Someone with great knowledge but whom everyone is afraid to approach for answers would be a 4. Someone who hoards knowledge to try to protect his or her bailiwick is a 4. Gone are the days when companies have the resources to tolerate this sort of selfishness.

A 3 is a team player who shows up for work every day, is cordial to coworkers, rarely complains, and gets the job done. Threes are pretty emotionally stable, but they not always consistent, and their inconsistency is the source of their Emotional Expensiveness. Every few months, a 3 will fall off his or her game by resisting change, making excuses for poor performance, venting an uncalled-for opinion, refusing to help with a project that "isn't my department" or support an initiative on which he or she consulted. Threes may have occasional meltdowns and have to be talked off a ledge, but only for what they see as good reasons. If this describes you, be very careful what you think you know for sure. Those quarterly meltdowns are costing you credibility.

Threes are very prevalent. Emotional Expensiveness is an everyday phenomenon. More often than not it comes from common feelings and behaviors such as wanting to be right, being judgmental, and believing that our success depends on someone or something outside ourselves. To some extent, we are all guilty. To the extent that we are honest about it, we have the power to change.

Someone with an Emotional Expensiveness rating of 2 has very little drag on the system. He or she is low maintenance and usually a pleasure to be with. Although this individual may not be taking excessive credit for her work, and may not be self-promoting, coworkers and managers recognize her contributions.

A 2 is someone who steps up quickly when there is work to be done. This doesn't mean she never asks questions about what to prioritize. It does mean she is a great risk mitigator when she sees a potential problem coming her way. Twos normally give the gift of their work freely while exacting no emotional cost from others. However, 2s are still on the path, working to evolve, because sometimes—maybe just a few times a year—even they get off track, get hooked emotionally or caught up in the rare drama before they even know what hit them.

I teach these concepts for a living and I am a reluctant 2. I have moments of frustration when I fail to use the tools I teach. I get mad and my staff get patient and go into problem-solving mode (because they're also 2s). The gate agents at Southwest Airlines might say I go as high as a 4 sometimes. I'm always working at this part of my Value Equation, but I can't say I'm a 1, and neither can most of you.

Ones are unflappable, able to stay neutral and focused in a variety of situations. They are very skilled at conserving energy that normally would go into drama and using it to have impact instead. It's not easy to become a 1 and even harder to remain a 1. It takes a daily practice of the many tools of enlightenment. Ones are so efficient and quiet about getting the job done, it's like elves came in the night. No one gossips about them because they seem to live in a drama-free zone. Ones are like unicorns, and are even more unusual than 5s, in my experience. A 1 has checked his ego at the door and worked to become self-mastered. When it comes to enlightenment and sheer Zen, 1s are right under Gandhi and Buddha.

Emotional Expensiveness Is Costing You

So, why should we keep trying if it is so hard to be a 1? Working on this number is the best way to improve your Value Equation. You need to give a lot in terms of performance and potential while taking very little emotional maintenance from others. You may give a lot, but if you're a big taker, you may be negating your contribution before it hits the bottom line. On the many occasions when I've been in on talks around impending layoffs, the employees who sign up and show up and say "Yes" the most often are the keepers. These are not necessarily the people whose names are heard in the hallway, but they are well known in the corner office and the Human Resources suite where the decisions get made. People who lose out in these situations are the ones who are Emotionally Expensive and come to work with loads of conditions. Don't let that be you!

Believe me when I say that good things come to those who are Emotionally Inexpensive. They are magnets for jobs, promotions, raises, and opportunities of all kinds. What would your life be like if you could eliminate the drama? I'm going to let one person's story speak for itself. Carol's story is a cautionary tale, but in the end it shows how attending to this number can turn your career around.

Carol learned early on, from her mentor in customer service, that a poker face is vital. A customer or employee should never see you flustered. She learned not to show any reactions, just as you wouldn't freely share your opinions about how your company is run with customers on the phone. But many of us don't realize that the same boundaries of professionalism apply with peers and senior-level staff as well. While she excelled in customer service because of her focus on staying neutral and keeping boundaries, Carol assumed that inside the company, and with some members of her team, she could vent or show her feelings of being rushed and overwhelmed. In fact, it worked to garner her coworkers' support and sympathy at times, and support and sympathy are easy to confuse (and often substitutes for) a strong professional relationship.

As Carol moved up the organizational chart and her duties became more demanding, her dramatic ways began to take a toll on her perceived value in the company. While no one told her at first, the tide was turning at her organization, and people everywhere were becoming less willing to excuse her Emotional Expensiveness. She gained a reputation as a drama queen that outshone her current results, and she could no longer rest on her past achievements. Results were now a basic expectation, not enough to set her apart in the company. A new team of leaders was looking for value, not performance at any cost. Carol said, "My first clue that something was wrong came when I and two other VPs were given a new supervisor. The two others got the same supervisor—a senior executive. I was told to report down the chain of command to someone else—actually, someone I knew quite well and considered a friend. I felt comfortable asking her, 'Hey, what's the deal? Didn't the SVP want me as a direct report?' I was half-joking, but my new supervisor became serious. 'Carol,' she said, 'drama comes with you.' Until that moment, no one had ever said anything like that to me. I was popular at work and had good relationships. I habitually ignored office politics because I felt people should—and would—take me as I am. Slightly chaotic, open and empathic to a fault, but truly good at my job. Suddenly, it had begun to appear to me that management didn't care for my style or the image I was projecting."

Carol's credibility was eventually so eroded that her numbers could no longer protect her, and she was let go. The rules had changed and no one had told her. She thought sharing personal issues and her daily struggles to meet her schedule and challenges were a "work right" and endeared her to others as a sign of her authenticity and humanness. But value became king in the organization, and her value waned. Her drama cost her a lot—and many more of you are unwittingly sabotaging yourselves in similar ways.

I worked with Carol to understand the New Value Equation and to realize the intense impact Emotional Expensiveness can have on one's value. She worked to better her number. Her day of reckoning came and after the initial shock, she stepped up and grew into her new reality. She has gone on to adopt many of the practices recommended in this book and is living within the new rules. She's landed her dream job as a consultant and has more flexibility in her schedule. She says, "Before I had no filter. Everyone knew everything about me. Now, as a consultant, my credibility is my livelihood. My job holds me accountable now. I'm in a great place. I hope others will recognize themselves in my story, and not have to go through what I did in order to learn the cost of Emotional Expensiveness."

I admire Carol's candor and her willingness to share her story here. It is not easy to be honest about Emotional Expensiveness. And to the extent that you have an attraction to drama, you may not necessarily see this for the problem that it is. But drama is never free. What is it costing you?

Rate Your Emotional Expensiveness

As honestly as you can, rate yourself on a scale of 1 to 5 for each of the following signifiers of Emotional Expensiveness. On this continuum,

1 = Never
2 = Rarely (once or twice per year)
3 = Sometimes (every couple of months, or less)
4 = Often (monthly)
5 = Daily

Remember to base your ratings on your actions, not your intentions.

1. I share my opinions regarding others' decisions and behaviors.
2. I need frequent encouragement to stick with a difficult task.
3. I tend not to be happy with my work until it has been praised by someone else.
4. I meet feedback with defensiveness or dismissiveness.
5. I believe I'm entitled to my opinions at work.
6. The way I'm feeling usually comes through loud and clear to my colleagues.
7. I spend as much time talking about my employer and colleagues as talking to them. I have good days and bad days at work.
8. I only support what I've been consulted on.
9. When I get angry at work, I express it either directly or through passive-aggressive behavior.
10. I share my personal and family problems at work.

Now, add your answers together and divide by 10.

Think you have your final result for the Value Equation? Not so fast. . . . Because Emotional Expensiveness is, by definition, something that affects other people, you aren't just reducing your own results; you are stealing time and energy from everyone around you. The true cost of an emotional outburst, or a bitch session in the cafeteria, or snapping at a coworker is higher than its cost to you. In fact, its cost to you is just the beginning. That is why you must take your Emotional Expensiveness rating and multiply it by 3.

Don't panic. Because Emotional Expensiveness counts for so much in the New Value Equation, working to lower this number is the single most effective thing you can do to improve your value

71

and your overall satisfaction with your work and life. To that end, I am going to spend the rest of the book teaching you to do just that.

Before we move on, plug in your numbers for Current Performance, Future Potential, and Emotional Expensiveness, then calculate your current value.

Rate Yourself with the New Value Equation

Your Value = Current Performance + Future Potential − 3 × Emotional Expense

$$\underline{\hspace{2cm}} = \underline{\hspace{2cm}} + \underline{\hspace{2cm}} - 3(\underline{\hspace{2cm}})$$

If you have a positive number, I congratulate you. Some of you will be positive—you are the reality lovers, the drama diffusers, the sane, high-value players. The time has come when you will get your just rewards, and you will soon be surrounded by fellow workers who are just as effective and happy as you are. You can actually multiply value with your number by diffusing the drama of others. You neutralize caustic people and negate their costly behaviors. You are a role model for techniques and behaviors that create top value. You call others to greatness by your calm, nonreactive mode and by your example.

If you have come up with a negative number for value, congratulate yourself for being honest. By facing your reality, you will improve. If you are looking at a negative value right now, know that you are far from alone. In fact, 83 percent of those who have been receiving high performance ratings scored negative numbers when first evaluated with the New Value Equation.

What if you're a zero? If you are used to being a 5 in the old system, it can be hard to be proud of your zero in this new system, in which even a 1 or a 2 is a rock star. If you are a zero, rest assured it's actually a great number and a great starting point. It's far better to be a zero who is fully accountable for how she got there than a 5, or even a 3, who is deluding herself. In fact, Zeros are some of the happiest and most peaceful people out there.

From this neutral place of zero, you can go on to add real value by focusing on improving yourself and not your circumstances. Imagine going home at the end of the day feeling great—knowing that you and your employer are even. You leave feeling pride in the work you did, confident that you served well, did your best, lifted people up, and added little drama or strife to the workplace. You gave your best, which is getting better all the time. You are energized by the difference you made, the impact you had, and by what you learned. You don't feel guilty for not having done a good job or for having sold out or belittled a coworker. You have given freely of your gifts, no strings attached. No negative feelings, just gratitude and pride. Your employer is thrilled as well, feeling that you performed well, you're a good deal for the present and a great bet for the future, as you grow and continue to learn.

In the New Value Equation, numbers go into negative digits really quickly because of the high cost of Emotional Expensiveness. If your number is deep in the negative digits, and you're tempted to put this book aside and ignore the New Value Equation, keep this in mind: When people get fired, or choose to leave a job that isn't working out, they take their problems along with them. If your number is very low, you may be having problems that are self-created. You owe it to yourself to master them before you move on. Those problems are there to teach you something, and until you learn it, you will never have peace at work. Whenever our beliefs are interrupted, we become uncomfortable and our first instinct is flight. But I'd rather see you address your challenges head-on and change your attitude. Getting Emotionally Inexpensive is not a quick fix, but it is the best way to improve your Value Equation.

In Part Two, I give you five rules that will make you not just Emotionally Inexpensive, but happier and more successful. Each of the next five chapters will get you a step closer to a number you can be proud of. We are moving toward a future in which Emotional Inexpensiveness is more valuable than any other attribute in the workplace. Bottom line: When you are a resilient, personally accountable employee who freely gives your talent and is willing to support the organizational direction without drama, you are a great deal and you are the one companies are looking to hire. You are raising the bar for those around you, and your impact far outweighs your cost. If you're not there yet, I can show you how to get there. Part Two is the blueprint for your future.

The Five Reality-Based Rules of the Workplace

Now that you have your number and know which areas you need to work on to improve it, let's get started. In Part Two, I discuss the Five Reality-Based Rules of the Workplace—what they look like in action, what you stand to gain by putting them into practice, and practical strategies for application. I show you how improving your Personal Accountability will make you happier and better at your job; why most people spend two hours each day suffering, and how to reclaim those hours for yourself; how to take action when you're tempted to quit; how to become energized and inspired by change, the one constant in every workplace; and secrets for creating great working relationships and overcoming common barriers to success, so you will love your job again. With my Reality-Based strategies and exercises, you'll not only boost your value and your employability, but you will restore peace and sanity to your life and to those around you.

4

Rule #1

Your Level of Accountability Determines
Your Level of Happiness, so DON'T HOPE
TO BE LUCKY. CHOOSE TO BE HAPPY.

Phil, a salesperson and one of my clients, was on the brink
of losing his job. His sales were down because, he said, his
customers' budgets had been slashed and product development
refused to develop cheaper products. Adding to his problems, his
company was setting outrageous goals despite the poor economy
and not informing him until half the sales period had passed. He'd
spent a great deal of time trying to get his boss to understand that
his low figures weren't his fault. After all, hadn't he been a top
salesperson for years?

This scenario has become all too common. Many of you feel
that you are working hard but are being undermined by others or
by factors outside of your control. If you are a typical employee, you
tend to handle it in a few predictable ways. First, you commiserate
and take a BMW (Bitching, Whining, Moaning) drive with your

77

colleagues, which can feel really good in the moment, like a team-bonding exercise, only voluntary. You get your frustrations out and end up with a list of reasons why, you all agree, you can't succeed and you aren't happy:

"Sales are down because of the economy."
"Our bosses don't listen to us."
"Our jobs are too big and too demanding."
"There's not enough time."
"There's too much bureaucracy."
"We're being micromanaged."
"We don't get the support/resources/information we need."

The next thing that tends to follow—once you've made a list of issues—is you take your list to your leaders, those you think can change your circumstances, or get you what you need: more staff, better technology, more time, clearer priorities, more understanding, more mentoring, more predictability.

Those of you who are less brave don't approach your leaders directly, but instead wait for your company's yearly engagement or satisfaction survey and let them have it, listing what parts of your reality they need to change in order for you to do better work. This is to little avail. Even your best, most understanding leaders can't always come through with everything you need and want—and those are the ones who are trying. You end up feeling discouraged, like you're being set up to fail. You do what you can, knowing that it may not have the impact you hoped for. Your happiness wanes, and you try to care a little less and accept what you can't change.

When you feel powerless, complaining or blaming your circumstances, leaders, or coworkers brings temporary relief, and it's a natural response to the frustration so many employees feel. You keep hoping for things to get better and for your luck to change. Instead, your jobs are growing and your impact is shrinking, and your leaders don't have all the answers. When you can't change other people or your reality, sometimes it may seem like your only option is to step down and make up excuses for why you had to. Right now, you are very likely blaming your leaders and your circumstances for your misery. They are similarly blaming you for your poor results. But it isn't your circumstances that are to blame. The root cause of everyone's dissatisfaction is lack of Personal Accountability and lack of understanding of accountability's true connection to both results and happiness.

Personal Accountability is the belief that you are fully responsible for your own actions and their consequences. It is a choice, a mind-set, an expression of integrity. While some individuals possess a higher natural inclination toward Personal Accountability, it can most definitely be learned, and it is not only the foundation for all success in work and in life but also a prerequisite for happiness.

Your challenges are real—you're not imagining them—but they don't need to become your excuses. We all want to see our efforts produce great results. You will get results when you stop complaining and blaming and focusing on what is happening "to" you, and focus instead on what you can do within your current reality, and with your current challenges, to compete, to deliver, and to succeed.

People who are accountable have an internal motivation to succeed, no matter what their obstacles. It starts with a commitment to do whatever it takes to get the job done. People with this quality are naturally the happiest and most engaged. Companies with the most engaged employees tend to be the most successful, but your engagement has to come from within you. It's a by-product of accountability, not a condition your leaders can create for you.

Without a foundation of accountability, engagement fluctuates like the tides, rising and falling with the fortunes of the organization and the moods of its employees. Many companies have gotten off track by focusing on trying to raise your engagement when they should have been working with you on your accountability. As a result, many of you have come to believe that it is your leaders' job to perfect your circumstances in exchange for the gift of your work. You've learned to ask for more resources and make lists of what you lack instead of taking responsibility for your own results. Many of you are trapped in the mind-set that your success and happiness is dependent on others and are finding both elusive. In this chapter, I show you how you can step up in new ways and reclaim that responsibility for yourself.

Personal Accountability will deliver the happiness and engagement you want and the success your organization needs. Today's accountability is the best predictor of tomorrow's results. Recruiters and human resource types have learned the valuable lesson that they can train accountable people to do almost any job. Hire the right people and they will bring their own motivation and engagement to everything they do. Be one of those people, and you will ensure your job security—or that your résumé goes to the top of the stack. If you work in a highly skilled profession, my message to you is that your skills alone are not enough to get you ahead anymore. Which brings me back to Phil, the salesperson whose job was at risk.

Phil was focusing on why his sales were down, why increasing them was impossible. I asked him to change his focus from why he could not increase sales to how he could, and what that would take. Phil's progression from reasons and excuses to possibilities started with that simple shift from "why" to "how." How could it work, right now, with the constraints he had listed?

Phil said that in order to sell high-priced products to people with less money, he would have to completely change the way he sold. His tone of voice made it clear that this was an outlandish concept to him. But he quickly realized that he had not changed the way he sold in more than ten years, and that worried him enough to convince him to try some new tactics. We got to work making a list of possibilities, and he found he had a lot of options he hadn't considered before. He could talk value, not price. He could talk "solutions," not products. He could get really great at helping his customers realize that they couldn't afford to waste their limited funds on an inferior product, that the obvious choice was to go for quality. Phil started to feel better, more hopeful, more influential in a situation in which he had felt embattled and victimized just an hour before.

What about the problem of getting his sales goals late in the season? How could he make that work? He would have to go full-out from the beginning, stacking the deck in his favor by having such a full pipeline that no matter when the goals were issued, he would not be caught short. As we talked, he admitted that the goals were always pretty predictable—higher than the previous year. They had only been coming as a shock to him because they exposed how far his numbers were from expectations and how hard he would have to work to make up for his lackluster performance to date.

Phil would have to make some big changes, but he saw how he could succeed, even with his difficult circumstances. There were examples all around him, some at his company and some working for the competition, winning contracts he was losing. He realized that all the successful salespeople he knew were working under the same constraints he was. If they could make it work, why couldn't he?

You can have all the talent in the world, but it won't be a productive talent unless you develop Personal Accountability. True happiness and engagement flow from this mind-set. You realize that you are the architect of your life, and that you can handle whatever comes your way.

Learned Helplessness: The Opposite of Personal Accountability

One of the best ways to understand Personal Accountability is to recognize and comprehend its opposite—Learned Helplessness. Learned Helplessness is when you believe you have no hand in your outcome. It is out of your control. An example that often resonates with my clients is the story of my hypothetical thyroid problem. For many years I worked in health care, where ironically there was very little healthy food available. I also had four babies, discovered Twinkies, and one day in my thirties I woke up "suddenly" overweight. It's amazing what can happen to us in just a few weeks, right? I tried a few diets, but nothing was working, so I went to my doctor because I had become convinced, thanks to WebMD, that there was something wrong with me. I must have a thyroid condition that was slowing down my metabolism and preventing me from losing weight.

When I went in for my test results, my doctor said, "Good news! There's nothing wrong with your thyroid—in fact, you're perfectly healthy." But I was devastated! Because I had Learned Helplessness about my weight. I was waiting for the doctor to give me the miracle pill that was going to fix my problem. If there was no problem, that meant diet and exercise.

I gave myself a great excuse for why I could not lose weight, when actually, if I was honest with myself, I had only ever been half-hearted in my attempts. I followed Weight Watchers, but only Monday through Thursday. I did NutriSystem, but I assumed wine was allowed because when I was introduced to the diet, they never mentioned it and neither did I. It turned out I was entirely responsible for my results. If I had approached the problem with that mind-set from the beginning, I wouldn't have put myself in the bizarre situation of praying for a chronic disease.

Too many of us live in a state of Learned Helplessness, believing that none of our problems is our own fault. We have no influence on our circumstances. We make half-hearted attempts to change things, get poor results, and then go back and rewrite history in our favor. "I tried so hard to get that promotion, but the boss plays favorites." "I wanted to win that bid, but there is so much politics and backbiting in this business, nothing I could have done would have made a difference." "If my diet's not working, I must have a disease." Personal Accountability cannot coexist with Learned Helplessness.

How Accountable Are You?

Personal Accountability is present in all of us to varying degrees, the product of both nature and nurture. Many of us have blind spots around our own accountability. Although we are not trying to be dishonest with ourselves, we find it far easier to call out others' failures in this area than to be self-aware. That's partly because most of the talk about accountability is about who is to blame, who dropped the ball, or whose butt is on the line. It is ironic that we tend to focus on others and what they should have done or prevented, placing ourselves in the role of the victim, because accountability is personal, and it is very empowering.

Personal Accountability is comprised of four factors:

1. *Commitment:* The willingness to do whatever it takes to get the results you desire

2. *Resilience:* The ability to stay the course in the face of obstacles and setbacks
3. *Ownership:* Unwavering acceptance of the consequences of your actions, with zero blame or argument, whether working individually or collectively
4. *Continuous learning:* Using both success and failure consciously as fuel for future success

How do you know if you are falling short in accountability? Notice what happens when you succeed. We tend to attribute success to our intelligence, skill, and hard work—not luck or circumstances. We don't say, "Wow, everyone made that really easy for me—they set me up to win." But what happens when you don't succeed? If you find yourself attributing failure or shortfalls to conditions you couldn't control, or to your boss or coworkers, or to a lack of resources or luck, that double standard shows low accountability. Accountable people have a healthy sense of pride in their successes and can account for the choices and behaviors that lead to success as well as failure.

Four Factors of Personal Accountability

There are four factors that contribute directly to your level of Personal Accountability. We explore each in detail, show you examples of the four factors in action, and give you specific ways to increase your own Personal Accountability.

Factor #1: Commitment

Committed people are willing. They lean into challenges and do what it takes to get the results they committed to, even if they don't have all the information or resources they think they need.

When you are committed, you buy in readily to what is asked of you. What you say and do reflects your true feelings. You are authentic in your interactions with others. There is no sarcastic or resentful inner voice keeping up a running monologue in your head.

If you want to show commitment, focus less on your job description and more on your larger role in the organization. Your job description is just someone's best guess at what you might do some of the time while employed in your company. This is the difference between saying, "I am willing," and "I'm willing if . . . it's my department . . . I am consulted in advance . . . I don't have to do more than my fair share . . . Others are also held to the same standard. . . ." Your role is to do whatever it takes to get the desired results, whether that's delighting a customer, fulfilling an order, selling a car, or handling a complaint.

I worked with Angela, a secretary at a shipping company. Shipping is an industry fraught with uncertainty, and schedule changes are a fact of life. But there is not one customer who expects or relishes getting news of a rerouting or a delay. When Angela started at the company, she was told that one of her duties would be to inform customers of service failures. But she quickly realized that these e-mails did not go out into a void. Customers whose shipments were late would often get angry and e-mail or call back. Angela was willing to inform customers of delays, as long as they took the news well, but as soon as they got upset, she would panic and quickly forward their messages to her boss. Soon her boss was up to her neck in irate customers and didn't have time to do her own job. Angela wanted her boss to take the angry customers off her plate and spent most of her time in defense mode.

Angela's job may have been simply to inform customers of delays, but her role was to go beyond just delivering the news, to satisfy and retain customers in spite of the delays. Angela stepped up,

85

got capable, and developed a plan for dealing with angry customers. She now adds a ton of value by representing the company professionally, listening to customers' frustrations, empathizing, and helping to solve their problems and restore their confidence in her company. While this requires more from her and benefits her organization, Angela benefits as well by being able to develop and practice customer service skills, a great avenue to her next promotion. There has been a big change in Angela since she took accountability for her least favorite part of her job. She's gained a lot of confidence and no longer has reason to fear her in-box.

Angela's was the challenge of a new job, but if you have been in the same job for years, it is easy to become complacent and believe that there are no new challenges out there for you or that you aren't "allowed" to go further than your job description. Look for opportunities to show your commitment and willingness. When faced with an opportunity to do something extra, step up and seize it. Instead of lamenting your situation, ask yourself, "What will add value in this situation?" Then go do that, even if it seems beyond your job description or carries a risk of failure. If you feel really safe all the time or, worse, bored, chances are you're not taking enough risks. You may be waiting for someone else to define what success means for you. Or you may be overfocusing on what other people need to do to improve your circumstances rather than taking action yourself. What is your level of commitment? How can you get more willing? Are you in, or are you out? Take off your conditions and get willing to do whatever it takes to deliver the required results.

Factor #2: Resilience

When you are resilient, you feel calm, purposeful, and confident in your ability to produce results regardless of your circumstances. Throwing up your hands and quitting at the first obstacle, or resorting to excuses, is not an option you consider. You are tenacious, and you bounce back quickly from setbacks. If you say you have "tried" to do something, you tried a dozen or more options, you persisted and were creative. ·

If you think back to your first job, chances are you will recall a near-universal experience: messing something up. The first time this happened, you may have felt perfectly justified in going to your boss with the story of why you didn't succeed: "I couldn't print the letter because the printer was broken." Circumstances beyond your control prevented you from accomplishing the task. End of story, right? Not so fast.

Depending on how tough your boss was, this sort of excuse may or may not have provoked a kind or forbearing reaction. What you soon learned was that the further you go up the chain of command, the less room there is for excuses. Deep down, your boss could not have cared less if the printer was broken. As far as she was concerned, it was your responsibility to print the letter, not to come to her with reasons why it wasn't possible. You may have resolved to be more resourceful next time. A broken printer, it turned out, had everything to do with you. Over time, you most likely learned to solve problems without involving your boss whenever possible and to get your work done in spite of minor setbacks. That's one way to become resilient, but you should take it further. Resilience is the fuel that powers accountability.

Resilient people are great, proactive problem solvers. Andrew worked for a company where internal communication had broken down. The company had expanded internationally and had so many employees that the right hand didn't know what the left was doing, and when someone needed to solve a problem for a customer, it was nearly impossible to figure out whom to call. It was a constant source of Learned Helplessness for people. They would put off dealing with even simple problems because the idea of calling ten colleagues who would forward the call to ten more, all without results for the customer, was too daunting. Andrew was in a meeting, listening to people complain about this problem yet again and speculate on whose job it was to unravel it.

Andrew refused to let this problem defeat him. He stepped up and created a big flowchart—a pivot table in Excel—to show how all the departments related to one another and what each was responsible for. He gathered information by calling colleagues, all of whom were happy to help when they heard what his idea was. It took him about fifteen hours in total, but it has saved his colleagues hundreds of hours and enabled connections that would not have been possible before. While everyone else was blaming others for the problem, he solved it. This task was not in his job description; it wasn't in anyone's, and that was the problem. Between your job description and your company's needs, there is a world of opportunity for you to seize.

Is there a problem that needs solving in your organization or just in your immediate sphere of influence? Is there a new idea you would like to pursue? Quit hoping someone else will come through. Think through what you hope to accomplish and how you will measure your results. Ask your supervisor for the challenge. How you frame any discussion with your supervisor will depend entirely on what the culture is where you work, but even in a very informal workplace, it pays to have done your homework so that your supervisor will see that your request for new challenges is serious and that you are not putting the onus on anyone else to develop your talent. Before you go to your supervisor, be sure your proposal is framed as "what I can do" rather than what others need to do to solve the problem.

Resilience is a learned skill, not some lucky genetic condition. You learn resilience every time you face a challenge, big or small, instead of stepping down and blaming your circumstances. Anytime you are stressed and unhappy, change your approach. Instead of looking to be bailed out, move through. You also can learn resilience by witnessing the resilience of others. Study those people who seem to overcome difficulties easily. They might look like they have it easy, but they are probably just more resilient than you are, so learn from them. Share strategies that have worked for you as well. Every act of generosity will multiply the results of your learning and inspire your peers to do the same for you.

Factor #3: Ownership

When you are feeling true ownership, you're able to give the gift of your work unconditionally. You don't look to others to validate your efforts or to give you the motivation to do your job. No one else has the power—or responsibility—to motivate you. If you believe otherwise, not only are you giving away all your own power to have impact, produce results, and be happy, but you risk having an attitude of entitlement—not accountability. A key part of ownership is the ability to clearly identify your part in your results—accepting the gap between what you created and what was needed or expected. People who are high in ownership are those who are willing to "own" their part in the outcome, good or bad, without drama. So if you want to work on ownership, begin seeking out regular developmental and performance feedback to help you understand, and internalize, how your choices are affecting your results.

Even if your company has an institutionalized system of reviews, don't wait for that one time per year that you sit down with your supervisor. Be proactive. All it takes is a single question: "What is one thing I could do differently to improve my results?" Listen to the answer. Say "Thank you." Go work on what they told you.

Make a deadline for yourself and keep track of your progress so you can report back later. Then, ask the question again. You will be amazed at what comes of it.

Most successful people depend on trusted mentors to help them make sense of their working lives. There are a few ground rules for making the most of these relationships. You are responsible for asking for feedback and support—in other words, you have to put effort into the relationship instead of waiting for your mentor to fill you with wisdom by osmosis. When looking for a mentor, choose someone you know you can trust and admire, someone who will inspire you, while being very clear that no one else is responsible for motivating you. Choose someone tough enough to offer you rigorous, consistent feedback. Ask, "Can you help me?"

The person who thinks you look good in everything is not your most valuable shopping companion. Needless to say, your mother, your spouse, or your best friend is not someone you want as a mentor. Just a tip: Stop using dinner time as BMW/mentorship time.

You must learn how to accept feedback, without ego or defense, as the gift that it is. This was a particularly challenging thing for me, and if it is for you, fear not. If I can do it, you can do it. Have you ever noticed that when you have a hard time accepting feedback—when you find you can't respond neutrally—it tends to be true? I know that the things I most need to work on are the things I tend to get the most defensive about.

One of my readers, who is quite perceptive and well read, likes to say that Dale Carnegie wrecked feedback forever with his "praise sandwich" concept. The idea is that you buffer negative feedback by beginning and ending with something that the individual has done well. The inevitable result is that we tend to focus on the positive things that were said first and last and ignore the gristly meat of the praise sandwich. The message is lost.

Your colleagues and managers owe you the truth, and vice versa. But you can't expect them to be up-front with you if you react emotionally. Stop taking everything personally. Feedback is about your work and your approach, not about you. Get analytical instead, and extract that which is useful and helps with development, regardless of how it is offered. Even if you have a boss you regard as hypercritical, it doesn't mean that his or her every criticism is automatically wrong.

Don't worry if, inside, you are slightly freaked out about what you are hearing. You get to go away and think it through, even have an emotional response if that comes up for you, before you consider your next move forward. All you need to do in the moment is say, "Thank you." If you're not feeling it yet, it's okay as long as you don't slam the door. Feedback is too valuable to jeopardize with an ill-considered response. It's always better to think it through on your own, then return when you are ready to have a constructive conversation.

Don't fear negative feedback. Instead, see it as the first step on the road to becoming happier, more accountable, and better at your job. If you can own up to the improvements you need to make, and make them, your pain goes away, blame disappears, and you raise your number and your impact.

If your boss is not forthcoming, you will have to try a bit harder, as Olivia, a participant in one of my workshops, reported: "My manager is not great at critical feedback. While I would like to believe that 99.9 percent of what I do is excellent, it probably isn't true. If I weren't meeting her expectations, she might not be open about it. So I have been in the strange position of trying to extract negative feedback from her, and I've developed some good strategies. When we have a meeting after an event, I usually will come right out and tell her what I think could have gone better, and what I plan to do differently the next time. I will ask her questions like, 'What's one thing you wish had gone differently this week?' or 'What can I expand on to do [some part of my job] better?' It was tough at first but I know I need her help—and her critical feedback—to grow as a professional."

Most managers do not enjoy giving negative feedback. It is a frequent subject in my one-on-one coaching. If you receive feedback in an open and calm manner, your manager will be more likely to be honest with you in the future, and your career prospects and development will be on a faster track as a result.

One of my favorite success stories in this area is a client I'll call Jane, who works in the transportation industry. She told me, "Whenever my boss would come to me with feedback, I would have my hackles up before he could even explain the problem. What I was thinking was, 'I work *so* hard for you. How can there be an issue?' Before in my career, my response would have been to go away saying to myself, 'He's crazy. He just doesn't know what he's talking about.' But now I tell myself he would not take the time and make the effort if he didn't care, if he didn't want me to improve my skills and further my career. I can and do grow from negative feedback now. Besides, when I became more calm and actually listened, I could tell he was actually very nervous to tell me when things weren't going right. He didn't enjoy it any more than I did. Now, he actually practices on me. He knows I'm 'safe'—not going to cry, not going to pick a fight. And he feels freer to tell me what is going on in our department."

Factor #4: Continuous Learning

Doing great work is not about never making mistakes or failing. It's about making sure those mistakes have the minimum impact

92

on those you serve, and that your failures inspire and inform new strategies in the future.

Developing this perspective takes some maturity, but it is its own reward. When you learn not only from your successes but also your failures, it transforms failure from something you are afraid of, which you must avoid, into something you can use to get better results in the future. No one ever has succeeded without some failures along the way, and holding back out of fear of failure guarantees you nothing but a lifetime of caution and restraint. A commitment to continuous learning is one of the main benefits I'd like you to take away from this book. Even when a meeting or a project doesn't go as well as you hoped, there is always a positive way to integrate it into your story. But it requires action on your part.

If you have made a mistake, or not delivered the desired results, the Personally Accountable way to handle it is to admit it without making excuses and work on the solution. Once you have done damage control, it's time to account for your actions. Resist the urge to give reasons, stories, and excuses. Whenever you insist on assigning fault, blame, or guilt, or shrug away from the lessons in your mistakes with glib apologies ("my bad . . ."), you rob yourself of the chance to turn your failures into lessons and new behaviors and to reflect on the themes that emerge in your life. So instead, reflect on the choices that you made and their impact on your results. What are three things you could have done differently that would have had a positive impact on your outcome? When you account for the competencies that you need to get better results, you can develop them—and your ability to respond differently to similar situations in the future.

If you are tempted to complain or slip into a victim mentality, watch your language. Practice speaking in an accountable way by using the pronoun "I" in short, simple sentences. The point here is to focus on what you, personally, did or did not do that led to your results—not to make yourself the subject of every conversation. The longer the sentences you are using and the more you talk about "they" and "me" instead of "I," the deeper you are likely sinking into reasons, stories, and excuses. Accounting honestly for your results ensures you will know how to handle things differently the next time, opening up myriad new options that didn't exist before.

Once I was interviewing a candidate for a job and I noticed a gap in his employment history. I asked him what happened and he said, point blank, "I was fired." He then told me the story of how he was fired—for cause—without a single sentence of blame or excuse. "I thought it was a good strategy to go over my boss's head when I disagreed with him. I talked poorly about him, went to his boss, sabotaged his plan, and engaged in gossip about him with my team. I did not take advantage of the opportunities he gave me to deal with him directly, and eventually, I was fired for insubordination." I was so impressed with his truthfulness and lack of excuses that I found myself was considering hiring him. He went on to say that he had learned a great deal from the experience. It was a wake-up call to him that he was being passive aggressive and that he needed to stop that and find ways to support that which he did not agree with. He told me I ought to hire him because he would bring a special talent to the team in addition to his skills. He could be instrumental in peer coaching his coworkers to be more direct with me as their boss. I did hire him, because I was impressed with his Personal Accountability. He'd mined his failure for lessons and committed wholeheartedly to working differently in the future. I liked his honesty, transparency, and resilience. Everyone will screw up sometimes. You don't have to be perfect. You do have to learn from your errors, and more important, capitalize on them.

You must get fearless about accounting for your results. For one thing, it saves you a lot of time and worry. Lacking the courage to face something is very time consuming and emotionally expensive. For another, it is essential to growth. Your development plans will spring directly from your work on accountability. Continuous learning is what will turn your development from a "have to" into a "want to." When you stop defending and blaming and see how you need to develop to be more successful, and commit to leverage that learning, your reluctance will turn to excitement.

Personal Accountability is something we all have to work on all the time. Each individual plays a vital role in building a culture of accountability within an organization. I work with chief executive officers on this rule, and I work with administrative assistants. And let me tell you, those admins are going somewhere fast. If you want to be indispensable, whether you work at a car wash or a Fortune 500 company, it all starts with moving out of the mind-set that everything is happening "to" you and into the mind-set that it is all happening "for" you. Notice how you feel when you are questioning "why" and when you're blaming others—in general, thinking like a victim. Notice how you feel when you are focused on how you can help and finding ways to make an impact. This is no accident. Your fast track to happiness is accountability. Feeling unhappy? Get accountable. Your level of accountability also determines your organization's results. Lacking results? Get accountable. Happiness and results are seconds away any time.

With Personal Accountability, you will look for opportunities, create better results and more good things will happen to you. To the uninitiated, it might look like luck. Bottom line: Victim mind-sets do not lead to success and happiness. Accountable mind-sets do, and luck has a much smaller role to play than most people believe. You will be credible in your business to the extent that people see you as Personally Accountable. If you want people to listen to you and invest in your future, this is the firmest foundation to stand on.

TAKE THE FAST TRACK BACK . . .
to Accountability

Are you feeling unhappy, disengaged, stressed, or frustrated?

Listen in on the questions you are asking, if only under your breath:

Why doesn't anyone tell me anything?
Why do things keep changing?
Why do I always have to make the coffee?

Questions that start with "why" or "who" are victim questions because they keep you focused on other people and arise from a worldview in which you have no power. To quickly turn from victimhood to accountability and take a fast track to happiness, rewrite your question. Replace the "Why" with "What" or "How" and focus on an action you can take, so your questions become:

What could I do to get the information I need?
What can I do to support the change?
How could I best serve myself and others?

The answers to these more accountable questions are your simple instructions—your marching orders. If you follow them, you will restore your happiness in just moments.[1]

Rule #2
Suffering Is Optional, so DITCH THE DRAMA!

It was a beautiful, sunny day in Mexico, and I was getting paid to lead people on a hike through a scenic trail. As far as I was concerned, it was a perfect day. My energy was high and my mood was buoyant. Then everything changed. Looking ahead on the trail, I saw something big and sort of squiggly on the ground. A snake! I started to freak out immediately. In my head I was reviewing the snakebite first-aid procedure, wondering how I was going to get twelve hikers safely around the snake—basically panicking. For the next few minutes, the hike, and my job, became grueling and exhausting as I worried about every eventuality while forcing myself to put one foot in front of the other. Until we got close enough to see that the snake was . . . a rope. What caused my suffering in that situation? It wasn't the rope—nothing in our reality actually changed, and we were never in danger—it was my perception, my dramatic assumption that the rope was a poisonous snake.

As humans, we regularly take ropes and make them into snakes. Especially at work. Most of you are not consciously trying to create drama, but unconsciously many of you do it all the time. When I worked as a therapist, here's how I fell into this trap: I would pull up the day's schedule of patients and think to myself, "What a packed, crazy schedule! I'll never get through it." That schedule was nothing more than information about the reality in which I was working that day, but instead of accepting it and just saying, "Good to know," I argued with my reality. I'd be tired before I even started.

Making ropes into snakes is very draining. If you find you are overwhelmed or stressed most of the time, you can be sure you are arguing with reality—an argument you will lose 100 percent of the time. The stress you are experiencing is not due to what is happening to you. It comes from the stories you are telling yourself about your situation.

The Third Column

The average person spends two hours each day in drama—complaining, creating stories, and arguing with reality. Surprised by that number? I was, too. I first discovered it by accident when I was conducting a time study to understand how physicians transitioning from voice dictation to online medical records would be spending their time between keyboards and patients. Our hope was that the new system would give them more time to focus on patients, but physicians themselves were convinced it would be less, not more. So we went to gather some data. Observers in each exam room were asked to document, in a two-column worksheet, how much time the physicians spent directly involved with patients, and how much time they spent typing. Soon after the study began, I got a call from the group to say my system wasn't working. They said they needed a third column to document how much time the physicians spent complaining about the keyboard to the patient. When the study was done, it revealed that the average physician was spending two hours of the day in drama—in effect, arguing with reality. I became fascinated with this phenomenon and went on to observe many other groups in other professions, finding out over time that this tendency to waste two hours each day on drama is almost universal. How big is your third column?

Most organizations are relentlessly searching for sources of waste in their processes, assigning teams to improve efficiency. Over time, eliminating even small sources of waste adds up to huge savings. Imagine what a hero you would be if you were able to recapture not only those two hours a day wasted on drama, but all the energy that the drama drains away? It is a huge opportunity.

When you get right down to it, there are only two ways to go through work today: with joy or with misery. Same work, same people—your choice. You can fight your reality and create drama, or you can radically accept what is happening and work within that reality to succeed anyway. Judging by the discontent in the workplace, it seems that many people have forgotten this very important truth: Your circumstances are what they are, but your reaction to them is up to you. In other words, your suffering is optional. Not only is your suffering optional, it is a source of drama that wastes time, saps your energy, and creates a toxic work environment for everyone. It is a waste of resources that are already in short supply. When you know about this incredible source of waste, how could you not work zealously to eliminate it from your day?

It's time to call a cease-fire on the war with Reality and enjoy the peace that ensues. Time to conserve the energy that used to be siphoned into drama and use it where it will have its highest return on investment—responding to the facts of your situation, the evidence in front of you. Rule #2 of the Reality-Based Workplace will restore your equanimity and calm, and your ability to live in the present, using your resources wisely. As drama becomes politically incorrect, the complainers and whiners who refuse to live by this rule will become more and more tired themselves, and worse yet, tiresome to others, hurting their chances and their results at work.

In this chapter, I show you where most drama in the workplace is coming from and give you simple strategies to end or avoid it. Drama is a choice—not a condition—and it is responsible for most of the negative emotions we feel daily. Yet these heightened emotions can be strangely addictive. Some people fear that if they ditch the drama, their workplaces will become robotic, devoid of humanity. In fact, the only emotions that disappear are the negative ones that were the result of flawed thinking. Positive emotions will return in abundance. Pride, anticipation, excitement, passion, joy, and jubilation are the direct results of the breakthroughs that happen when you ditch the drama.

So many organizations are calling for innovation as a new workplace competency, even naming it in their strategic plans. Unfortunately, many of them are stuck in the false belief that innovation is something they need to teach you. I am thrilled to have discovered that most of us are already innovative. It is our natural state when we are able to let go of the time and energy-wasting drama. At the end of this chapter, I give you some ways to tap into that creative energy.

A Bad Case of the Shoulds

The first major source of drama in most workplaces is judgment. Our minds are prone to judgment, and left unchecked, they will use it as a continual source of fuel. We tend to lead with our view of the world—who should buy the doughnuts and how often; how and when our bosses should consult us; how people should act in meetings; how they should clean up after themselves; how they should drive; how they should show their appreciation.

"This should not be happening" is another form arguments with reality often take. We are all experts on what "should" and "should not" be. If something happens outside the realm of our expectations, or wishes, we start to critique, complain, and defend our point of view instead of choosing a more productive reaction.

William, who worked in the shipping department of an electronic components manufacturer, was in one of my sessions, and I asked him what was causing him drama and frustration at work. Before the question was out of my mouth, his face clouded over, and he went on to describe the production line that put the finishing touches on each component before shipping.

They were incredibly slow—excessively picky, in his opinion. They held up shipping and caused delays that angered customers, and he was the one who had to explain and apologize. When he'd been in charge of that line, it had been super-fast and customers had never complained. I asked him how much of his day was spent focusing on that group and he said, "Probably about 80 percent." I asked him what he spent most of that time doing, and he admitted he was mostly judging and critiquing them, complaining about them to others, stewing while he did his work, and bugging them to hurry up. He was asking himself, "Why are they so slow? Who is going to take responsibility for this? When will the powers that be figure it out and step in?" Very frustrating, unaccountable questions that were getting him nowhere except deeper into the drama about why he was right and how things "should" be.

Would You Rather Be Right, or Happy?

If you want misery, stay connected to the belief that you are right—be the judge of the world. If you want happiness and efficacy, stop judging and start helping. I asked William, instead of judging the other employees on the line, what he could do to help the line go faster. He came up with a list of actions he could take: he could check the tracking software instead of interrupting them with questions; he could update the checklist he created while he was on that line to accommodate the newest products, and share it with them; he could share a technique he had learned in his days on the line that would speed up their decision-making process; and he could change the way he pulled product from the line. Some of these actions required more work on his part, but at least he'd feel he had some impact on the situation. It turned out there were a lot of actions he could take with the 80 percent of his day that had been given over to "shoulds."

I saw William a few months later, and he had a big smile on his face. The line was going faster, the customers were complaining less, and he felt great because his actions had contributed to that outcome in a way that his complaints never had. I asked, "Do you ever backslide?" And he said, "Yes, often. I'm my own worst enemy." Whenever he starts focusing on being right, or how things "should" be, his bliss ends. Luckily, he said, when that happens he asks himself, "Would you rather be right? Or happy?" And he chooses to forego scorekeeping in favor of peace. I asked, "Do you ever worry anymore about having to do more than your fair share?" He said, "Actually, I feel a bit guilty now that I have more than my fair share of peace and enjoyment at work."

So many times, we miss an opportunity to step up and be accountable because we're blinded by a mind-set of judgment. If a movie projector has a piece of lint on its lens, it will be projected onto the screen in every frame. It would be easy to conclude that the screen or the film is defective, when all we need to do is clean that dirty lens. You do your best problem solving from a place of neutrality where you can see all of your options clearly.

In our lives every day, events and people fall short of expectations. Try not to let it frustrate you too much. The space where you can add the most value is the space between reality and perfection. That is one great big space, in which you have infinite potential to make a difference. Becoming a lover of Reality is doing more than acknowledging that space; it's finding a way to inhabit it and use it to reach your highest potential. So don't hate the imperfection. It will be with us as long as we are human. Think of the vast space between reality and perfection as your opportunity to shine, to have value, and to make a positive impact. That space is why most of us are currently employed, so we should learn to embrace it.

The Monster Under the Bed Is in Your Head

The most peaceful life is one in which you are able to take things at face value, and yet few of us do. Instead, we speculate. We move away from the facts of a situation and make up a story.

103

We predict outcomes (usually negative) and base our actions on feelings rather than data. Instead of problem solving proactively, we suffer proactively.

I was visiting a client recently on a factory floor. A phone in the corner started ringing, and one of the employees ran to answer it. As he listened to the voice on the other end of the line, his eyes got big and he gave his supervisor a panicked look. Putting the caller on hold, he said, "That's the new VP of operations. He wants to know our total throughput for the shift and how many full-timers were on the line! Don't you think that's suspicious?" He went on to make up a drama-filled story: "They're looking to cut out our facility so they can move the work out of state. I've Googled this guy—his whole career has been all about busting unions and shutting down plants. It's only a matter of time until we are all out of a job." I was amazed at the incredible story he had crafted within thirty seconds of receiving this call. The supervisor joined in the drama and began to work with the employee on a response that would ensure the line looked as efficient as possible. All the while, the vice president waited on hold.

I stepped in to help—but not with the defensive response to the VP. These people were in a lot of pain, and I wanted to get them back into reality, where we could respond to the facts instead of anxious speculation. I asked the employee, "What do we know for sure?" hoping to get him out of his story and back to a solid foundation of fact. Each time he repeated part of his story, I gently challenged him, "Yes, but what do we know for sure?"

Finally, he admitted that all he knew for sure was that the VP was on hold and had two questions. Given that, what would be the next best thing action he could take? When we are operating in reality, the next action to take is usually pretty clear, as it was in this case. He said, "I could check the system and find out our throughput and number of full-time employees on the line and answer his question." The VP thanked him, and the day went on. But both the employee and the supervisor were really stressed for a while. What was the cause of their stress? Was it the VP's simple questions, or the story they were both believing about his motives?

The era of the drama king and queen has come to an end. We are no longer in need of town criers to share the stories of why things are screwed up, or who is to blame, or to point out why things aren't working or that the sky is falling.

Whenever you move away from the facts of a situation and let your imagination get the better of you, you move into defense mode, where your only options are fight or flight. When these anxious thoughts enter your mind and are left unchecked and unquestioned, they limit your choices. Your feelings, rather than evidence, begin to direct your actions. Why is it that dread and impending doom are our default position? What if our go-to position were neutral? Just to stick to the facts, respond with honesty, and trust that we are capable of adding value and handling what comes our way no matter what. What a peaceful way to live—no monsters under the bed.

I want you to absorb the fact that there are no innocent victims when it comes to drama. If your life is full of drama, you are its creator or its co-creator—not its magnet. The stress and unhappiness we feel is not the result of what happens to us. It is the result of the stories we tell ourselves about those events—stories we are literally making up in our heads, ascribing negative thoughts, motivations, and intentions to others that we cannot possibly know to be true.

105

Even if you don't share your drama with others, there is no such thing as a throwaway thought. Most thoughts lead in some way to an action—or lack of action. Your thoughts influence the way you act, and the world responds to what it observes. So even if you are not sharing your stories with others, your thinking manifests itself in a way that affects everyone around you and the way they see you.

The Facts Will Set You Free

You can become a Reality-Based thinker who deals in facts and evidence, not drama, by learning to recognize and edit your stories. One of my best-loved mentors, Byron Katie, teaches a series of questions that I was introduced to long ago.[1] Her clients have used these questions, which she calls "The Work," to overcome everything from emotional and physical trauma, to obesity, drug abuse, and more. Over the years and with hundreds of clients, I have created a similar set of questions that are based less on feeling and more on action—to help you get out of story and back to reality.

The magic of these five simple questions is that you can apply them to any situation in your life that has you worried. Answering these as honestly and thoroughly as you can will help you eliminate the thoughts that are the root cause of most drama in your life. You can return to the five questions any time you are feeling anxious or stressed or are having a hard time ditching the drama. You will learn to listen to your thoughts and discard any content that is not based in reality. Your stress will evaporate, and you will know what you ought to do next. Some day it may become as automatic for you as it has for many of my clients—a new habit of mind. Here are the basics.

Edit Your Story. Respond to the Facts.

Any time you begin to experience stressful thoughts and feelings about an event or another person, pause. Ask yourself:

1. What story am I telling myself right now?
2. What do I know for sure? (only the facts)
3. How do I act when I believe my story?
4. Without my story, what would I be doing to help?
5. What is the very next thing I can do to add value right now?

Try to answer these questions as specifically as you can. It may help to write down your answers. The answer to Question 5 is your Simple Instruction—the next best action you can take to eliminate your negative feeling and move forward in a constructive way. Do your work, find the simple instructions, and go do that.

The point of this exercise is to make sure you are responding to the facts of a situation versus your story (all of the thoughts you've made up about it). Our stories come from a deep, inner voice of doubt and dissatisfaction that wastes our time, causes us to feel helpless, and stops us from moving forward productively and getting the results we want. When the story is gone, all that remains is the final question, leading you directly to fearless action and tremendous value.

How you respond to a potentially stressful situation or person is a choice. Once you commit to embrace Reality, your choices will be much more conscious. By focusing on what is, rather than what you'd hoped for, what you'd prefer, or how things "should" be, you conserve energy that would otherwise be wasted. Holding on to this energy enables you to use it to affect your situation, to have a constructive reaction rather than a dramatic or destructive reaction.

107

One of my readers put it well: "Stop letting people live rent-free in your brain. Either let it go, or start charging them rent."

By way of illustration, here is an example of someone (we'll call her Cathy) I was coaching recently about some problems she was having with her boss. Here is how she articulated her problem to me:

"Cy, my new boss is really flighty, and when she feels ill prepared, she micromanages me. It is driving me crazy. Managers
shouldn't be that way."
"But this one is?"
"Yes."

From there, we started looking for a constructive solution to her problem. Cathy started with the first question:

1. What story am I telling myself right now? "I'm telling myself that my manager is flighty. I'm telling myself she should be better prepared and that she should trust me more. She should give me some notice when she wants me to come up with specific statistics for a meeting. She makes it appear like I am the one who isn't prepared. I'm telling myself she and I just do not get along, and I am not sure we can because we are like oil and water. I'm telling myself that having her for a boss is making my job harder and her management style is stopping me from feeling competent and doing a good job."

Cathy was able to answer the question thoroughly and articu- lately. I felt I got where she was coming from. But she needed to inquire further about this, because she was really feeling stressed, and that was a sure sign that she needed to separate her reality from her story about her boss.

2. What do I know for sure? (only the facts)

Next, we edited Cathy's story. We went through it line by line and inquired on everything she had said. What could we know for sure was reality?

"I'm telling myself that that my manager is flighty and unprepared."

What is the evidence?

"When we have meetings, she often goes on the attack and asks me all kinds of detailed questions. It makes me nervous. It embarrasses me in front of our colleagues when I don't know the answer off the top of my head."

So, Cathy felt that her boss was trying to cover her own lack of preparation by asking Cathy a bunch of random questions. This was ascribing a motivation to her boss that Cathy could not know for sure to be true. That part was Cathy's story. Reality so far: "She asks me questions in meetings and I am caught off guard and don't know the answer."

We moved on to Cathy's next statement:

"She should trust me more."

When you use the word *should* with regard to another person, most of the time you are dealing with story and not reality. We all feel we know how things "should" be, but few things in life are so black and white that everyone agrees about them. The "should" is part of Cathy's story.

"She makes me appear unprepared."

No one can "make" Cathy feel this way. It is not in her boss's power, even if she wanted to, to "make" Cathy look unprepared if Cathy is, in fact, prepared. This is Cathy's fear talking, not her boss's power over her. And her fear was coming from the story she was telling herself.

"She and I just do not get along, and I am not sure we can because we are like oil and water."

How long had Cathy known her new boss? A few months. They had never spent time together outside of work, and Cathy was not sure what they had in common other than their place of work. So she identified this as part of her story, since in reality it was unclear how she and her boss would get along in the future, and Cathy did not know for sure how her boss was feeling. Finally:

"Having her for a boss is making my job harder and her management style is stopping me from feeling competent and doing a good job."

By this point in our coaching session, Cathy was starting to see how it was actually her story about her boss that made her feel incompetent and that she was not able to do her job well. We were only able to extract two lines of straight reality from her answer to Question 1: "She asks me questions in meetings and I am caught off guard and don't know the answer. I fear looking unprepared."

Cathy's story was three times as long as her reality! And talk about stressful. So we put reality aside for a moment and Cathy asked herself,

3. How do I act when I believe my story?

"I get frustrated. I skipped our last meeting. I talk about her behind her back. I don't listen to her. I don't keep her up to date and informed, because I don't like meeting with her." At this point, Cathy smiled self-consciously. She had started to see who she was being in the context of this story and how she was co-creating her manager's behavior with her own behavior. As self-awareness dawned, the solution started to become clear. We moved on to Question 4, and Cathy asked herself:

4. Without my story, what would I be doing to help?

"I would be more proactive toward my boss. I would initiate meetings with her instead of skipping them. I would keep her up to date and informed without her having to ask." If Cathy wanted her manager to trust her more, she herself needed to be more prepared and more reliable.

5.   What is the very next thing I can do to add value right now?

Instead of arguing with reality, Cathy had figured out a way to deal with it. She would be proactive about filling her boss in before they went to meetings with their colleagues. Then Cathy would have the opportunity to find out in advance what her boss's questions might be and gather the necessary statistics before her boss put her "on the spot." She would appear—and be—prepared.

This exercise led Cathy to think about how she was managing up and try to get better at a valuable skill she'll draw upon throughout her career: being less Emotionally Expensive. Her Personal Accountability increased. She also gained incredible insight into the role she was playing in creating her situation by acting on her emotion and speculation. Learning to edit her story was one part of her process of continuous learning and development.

Even if the universe gives you a boss you see as flighty and micromanaging, you can learn something from that—not only how you may be contributing to the problem, but what you can do differently that will improve the course of your career and not just your current position. When you separate the facts from your story and respond only to the facts, it becomes surprisingly clear what your next best action should be. Get evidence based. You will be amazed how it simplifies your life. Notice how much more energized and grounded you feel when you use reality as your anchor and make an impact without wasting energy on drama. Low investment, high results—doesn't that sound like a profitable model?

Stay in Your Lane

There are three lanes in life: Lane 1, your business; Lane 2, other people's business; and Lane 3, Reality's business—everything from traffic to floods. If you remain in your lane, tending to your own responsibilities in the present, you will seldom be stressed. You'll be clear, capable, and effective. Stress enters the picture when you leave your lane to meddle in other people's business, judging or trying to control them. But the worst is when you take on the impossible task of trying to argue with, or change, Reality. This includes straying from the present into the past, to deal out blame and opinions about what already happened; or into the future, to imagine all that could go wrong. You will suffer every time you veer uninvited out of your own lane.

I worked with a team at an insurance company who were deep into drama. Their manager told me that it had reached a level where they could hardly talk to one another and very little work was getting done. "Our team was a soap opera. We spent all day telling stories about one another and assigning motives that weren't based in fact. I was spending most of my time trying to defuse this drama and it was on so many levels it was hard to know where to start. Just one example—my team was located on two different floors. One day I got an instant message from an employee upstairs, complaining that the employee in the next cubicle over had his e-mail alert set too loud. Instead of going over to him and asking him to turn it down, she was sitting there, stewing, deciding that he was doing it on purpose. She blew it up in her mind to such a degree that she felt the need to involve her manager. That is needlessly elevating a situation that should have been addressed between them."

This story is a great example of another way people turn ropes into snakes: attributing motives to others' behavior. We could not possibly know what is going on inside their heads, but that rarely stops us. The employee who was annoyed by her colleague's loud IM alert jumped right to the conclusion that he was doing it on purpose to annoy her when she could have applied some mental agility. There could be many other reasons behind his behavior—he is hard of hearing, he wears headphones and can't hear the alert on low volume, he doesn't know how to adjust the volume of the alert, he wants to hear it from across the room—none of which concern her directly. Notice how she acts when she assumes the worst about his motives: blaming, angry, tattling. How do you think that affects his feelings and behaviors toward her? Whereas giving him the benefit of the doubt and politely asking him to turn the volume down would have been a reasonable reaction. "*This* means *that*" will drive you crazy and take you off course every time. Giving the benefit of the doubt, not jumping to conclusions, is part of what it is to be professional.

Tim, an ad executive I know, told me how common it is for clients of his agency to call for changes at the last moment, even when they have had weeks to review a campaign: "This happens all the time. Once, a client wasn't getting back to us and we were sure she hated the design. She turned out to be on a long vacation. Many times, a client will call at 5 p.m. and request changes for the next morning. The temptation is to get livid. 'How could they treat us like this? It's unacceptable!' But you could spend half an hour having that conversation, whereas it would only take you a couple of minutes to make the changes and send them over."

Even worse than spending thirty minutes suffering over someone else's perceived lack of respect for your time is leaning over the next cube to draw a coworker into your drama, taking ten minutes of their time to tell the story so they can validate your outrage. Which is the bigger lack of respect for someone's time? At least the customer pays you.

During a presentation at Tim's office, I asked, "How many of you have felt underappreciated by a client in the last year?" They all raised their hands. "Who expects it to happen again?" Again, every hand went up. "So," I asked, "what's the point of getting mad when it happens? You expect it. You know it's going to happen. Save yourself the time it would take to get outraged and get home earlier."

Let Your Sane Response Determine the Outcome

Ultimate job security comes when you are adding more value than anyone else, and that involves checking your ego at the door, ditching the drama, and developing your understanding of how your responses to your circumstances determine your outcomes. I recently heard another great example of this in action. It came from one of my readers who had been working on lengthening her fuse at work: "Last week I got a nasty e-mail from an employee in another department. There was a time when I might have responded with sarcasm or anger myself, but I was practicing Reality-Based behavior—just looking at the facts. I didn't immediately assume that she was trying to be rude but gave her the benefit of the doubt. I didn't respond to her tone, and resolved her problem politely the best way I could. A few minutes after I hit "Send," the phone rang. It was this other person calling to say, 'Hey! I thought you were going to be nasty to me but you weren't—thanks!' It turned out she *had* actually meant to be rude to me, expecting to start something because she was having a bad day herself. She regretted it, especially when I responded professionally to her nasty e-mail. When I didn't take the bait, the whole thing was diffused and we could almost laugh about it."

When you embrace Reality, you will find you can fix many problems by changing yourself rather than continuing to suffer at the mercy of others' shortcomings. After all, people tend to respond with the same attitude with which they are treated. If not the first time, then over time. If you are withholding, your boss may be micromanaging. If you justify your behavior based on hers ("She is micromanaging and it frustrates me so I skip our meetings"), you may believe you are right, but you definitely won't be happy or successful.

Learn to see stress as a sign—not that the world is going to hell in a handbasket, but that you are not currently living in reality and need to inquire on your thinking. Imagine going home at the end of the day, and when your partner or kids ask you how your day was, just telling the truth—only the facts? Your narrative becomes pretty short! A far cry from the stories we usually tell. Teach your spouse and kids to inquire on their stories, and you may even get to eat your dinner in peace with no evaluations.

Steering Clear of Other People's Drama

Unfortunately, no matter how hard you work on yourself, it can be difficult not to be drawn into other people's drama. What do you do if the climate at your office is Emotionally Expensive, or worse, if the resident drama king or queen is your boss?

The first thing to remember is that everyone has got a story. When someone does something that seems weird to you, they are likely acting on a story and it might not be clear, even to them, exactly what that story is. But once someone gets into a story they are telling themselves about a person or a situation, they will seek to collect only information that supports it. They will forget that multiple things can be true at the same time, and that multiple

115

perspectives are valid, and go out looking for others to collude with them.

It takes a lot more effort to stay in denial of Reality than it does to embrace it and accept it. Plus, if you insist on fighting Reality, you will have to hang out with other people who are doing it, too. They'll be your closest companions as long as you are as negative as they are. Talk about bringing your number down. Nothing good comes out of that box.

Once you are aware of this, you will start to see it coming from a mile away, often in the form of office gossip or complaining. One of my workshop participants had been feeling more relaxed at work after she realized that she is not obligated to internalize others' drama. "One member of our staff was frustrated because she didn't get the vacation days she wanted. She was expressing her frustration to everyone who would listen. It felt like she was trying to make it personal. Before, I might have taken it that way and become frustrated too. Now I feel more prepared to let it go."

Sometimes we excuse time spent gossiping at work, thinking of it as a break, or as something that helps morale. After all, don't we all have a right to a venting session now and then? That could not be further from the truth. Gossip is a morale killer, and break time should be relaxing and uplifting. Someone who worked for a large chain of stores shared with me that his team—so busy they did not have time to gossip—had the highest engagement scores in the company. "We were working longer hours than most—seventy-hour weeks—but we enjoyed working together and it was great. People were trying to join our team. We had no turnover, except promotions within the company, for five years. If a new team member would come in and want to stir up gossip, we'd let them know it wasn't how we operated. If you think about it, the hour or so you spend shooting the breeze adds up—five days per week, fifty working weeks of the year—that's 250 hours! Imagine what your career could be with that 'found' time."

You are never obligated to enter into another person's story. You can offer empathy ("I'm sorry for what you're going through"), which is not the same as sympathy (when you take on their emotional state as your own). One of my clients has a coworker who is extremely sympathetic. "If she gets to the office and hears that there was an accident on the highway during her commute, she will occupy the first hour of her day fretting about the victims and wondering if there was anything she personally could have done to contribute to it. Meanwhile, she is not present to what is going on in her immediate surroundings. Sympathy is a nice quality but it can be taken too far and tip over into drama." The cool thing about having separate bodies is that when others are in pain, you're not, and vice versa. You can be free to focus on adding value.

Offering empathy leaves you some distance from the other person's situation, which is appropriate at work. Remember, your colleagues have friends, relatives, parents, and children—they don't need you to fill any of those roles for them. Maintaining a distance doesn't feel natural to everyone at first. You may worry about coming across as cold, but that is preferable to getting sucked into other people's drama, which can be emotionally debilitating as well as stop your advancement. It is hard to get promoted when you are seen as one of the pack, so enmeshed with your coworkers that they would not be able to see you as an effective leader.

When other people come to you in drama mode, you can always say something noncommittal, like "Thanks for letting me know," or "Good to know." These cover a lot. Then you can change the subject. By having a noncommittal reaction, you make it clear that you don't judge the other person but you are not going to get into their story and collude with them. Lack of collusion kills drama; they will leave you alone and find someone else to listen to them. And you can find some more like-minded people to hang out with at work. You may even find some easy converts, and soon you'll be building a new culture, one cubicle at a time.

Here are some other effective responses to gossip and drama:

When someone is getting into a story: "I hear what you're worried might happen, but right now what do we know for sure? What are the facts?"

When someone is fear mongering or trying to shoot down someone else's plans: "I'm confident that if X happens, we can deal with it."

When someone is harping on the past: "I prefer to focus on what we can do in the present instead of what happened in the past or may happen later."

When someone wants to gossip about a coworker who may be struggling: "Really? What can we do to help him or her?" Kindness kills gossip. Someone who is expecting you to be mean with them will be completely foiled by this tactic.

If all else fails, distraction may be your best option. In my experience, most people who come to tell you their story do not want solutions. They just want to vent. But you have the opportunity to try to work through issues with others if they are willing. If they aren't, let them be. There is only so much you can do to help, and unsolicited help is usually not appreciated.

If you are often distracted by office drama, try to figure out what you are doing to attract that, and don't do it anymore. Are you passing on gossip that feeds the flames? Is going out for drinks with your coworkers on Friday nights resulting in information overload on Monday morning? Are you hanging out in the break room when what you really need is a walk outside in the fresh air?

Are you unconsciously holding the wool someone else is knitting into a story? If so, put it down.

If you have been one of the pack, participating in the office rumor mill or sharing lots of details about your private life at the office (or worse, over many cocktails after work), there is a way to pull back, and it's important that you do if you have ambitions beyond your current role. Your social life and your work life should be scrupulously separated. When you are with colleagues, only do things, wear things, and say things that would be appropriate in the office. If you make that one change—to get consistent in your behavior—it will go a long way to reestablishing your credibility.

You may not be able to change the world, but you can change your corner of it. What you will notice is that it no longer matters what others are doing or saying. Then you can go forth and find the willing with whom to work, and when your group starts producing great results you will be rewarded and listened to. Let the squeaky wheels go on making noise.

What Comes Next?

There is a big difference between jumping to negative conclusions about the future and using your precious time to decide what you would like to create and collaborating to accomplish it. When you ditch the drama, you will have time to dream again.

I first saw this in action at a dinner I attended during a workshop. Our homework, as a group, was to have a conversation that contained only the truth and the facts—no judgment, no evaluation, no speculation, and no analysis. At first it was very difficult. So much of what we say is laced with evaluation. Even saying "The stars are beautiful tonight" was off limits. What were we supposed to talk about? "There are 1.2 trillion stars in the sky" does not make for scintillating conversation. And it is practically impossible to talk about the past without lapsing into storytelling and judgment.

All of us got very quiet, until the group livened up with the realization that the future was ripe for discussion. One by one, we shared our hopes, our bucket lists, and our plans for how to improve our homes and our lives. One person wanted to do missionary work in Kenya. Another was excited about a home renovation project. A third hoped to go back to school and get another degree. Something amazing happened—others at the table started jumping in with ideas, suggestions, and connections that would help make these dreams a reality. Conversation and energy flowed freely as we all focused on what we could do to move each others' plans along.

Creativity is our natural state once we ditch the drama. Think of drama as the weeds choking a garden. Nothing else can flourish. When you get rid of the weeds, you can grow anything. No one needs to teach you, and there are a few things you can do to unleash it.

First, don't wait for inspiration to strike. Go track it down. Look outside your industry. Get exposure to great ideas by reading widely in books and online. Start a book club with your colleagues. Either read the same book and discuss it or read different books and give each other summaries of the best ideas you learned. Start a group in which each person follows three blogs and then reports on them to the others—you'll spend a little time and get a great return on your investment.

Movement forward begets innovation, so keep moving. If you have an idea and it's not perfect, start working on it. You don't know what will come of it. Keep an open mind to trying things that might not work. The key is to notice quickly when something's not working and try something different, and keep trying. Too many of us fail once and quit. If it doesn't work one way, instead of getting bogged down in the details, ask how it could work a different way and try that.

If you solve a problem or learn a new way to do part of your job, figure out who else in your organization would benefit from that knowledge and go share it. If you learn something, teach something. Get excited about learning, and have the attitude of a perpetual student. Be careful what you think you know for sure. When we think we're right about something, we quickly become righteous and all learning stops. Be willing to try anything that may serve the larger goals of your organization.

In the next chapter, you'll learn how to turn great ideas into reality by building fearlessly and wholeheartedly on your own and other people's plans. I show you why buy-in is not optional, and action, not opinion, adds the most value.

TAKE THE FAST TRACK BACK . . .
from Stress to Peace

Are you feeling stressed and anxious?

Let go of your "shoulds."
Stop judging and start helping.
Let go of the need to be right if you could be happy instead.
Ask yourself, "What do I know for sure?"
Edit your story down to the facts.
Figure out your simple instructions—what you can do next that will add the most value. Then go do that.

Without drama weighing you down, you will be free to make accountable choices, free of your stories and excuses, free of your and other people's drama. When you work from a place of neutrality, your instructions are simple, and you will have plenty of energy to carry them out and plan a great future.

Rule #3
Buy-In Is Not Optional. YOUR ACTION, NOT OPINION, ADDS VALUE.

I have the opportunity to work with many people in support roles, such as information technology professionals, whose leaders are seeking to change the mind-sets of their highly qualified employees from "order taker" to "solutions provider" so that they can bring more value to their organizations. Whenever I start working with a new group, I'm amazed at what lousy reputations many of these talented professionals have created for themselves. Their main role is support, and yet when I survey their internal customers, "nonsupportive" is the most common comment.

As I lay out the fact that their role is one of support, they are eager to give me reasons why those they serve don't deserve it. I've heard elaborate justifications why so much of what they are asked to do is not their job, starting with their opinion that the people who call them for help are incapable: technically underskilled, behind the times, basically idiots when it comes to computers and business IT systems. One woman stands out in my memory. She was extremely frustrated and came to me after our session, saying, "Cy, it isn't my job to teach every employee basic computer skills. Some of them can't even type. Others don't even keep track of their passwords, let alone use the system we developed to its full functionality."

You know what? She was probably right. (And if this describes you, you need to be doing a better job of keeping up with technology in order to stay relevant.) But what she was doing was not helping.

I asked her what she knew was the mission, the role of her department as a whole, and she said it was to ensure employees had the technology to facilitate their business goals and that they were getting the most out of it. Then I asked her what her individual role in this larger goal was, and that's when the light bulb went on. If the IT department's role was to help employees get the most out of the technology they were providing, employees' basic computer skills were not beyond her remit. Far from it.

Meanwhile, her opinions and editorializing—about how everyone should be tested for technology skills prior to being hired, and how the company was wasting money on IT systems that were over employees' heads—were stopping her from fulfilling her role at work. She was adding little value, and her Emotional Expensiveness was through the roof. She made people feel so stupid that they were afraid to call on her for support.

Somewhere along the line, she had lost track of what she'd been hired to do. When she went to work for her company, she agreed to provide a service and to work on behalf of the organization, furthering its agenda and supporting its goals. In order to do that, she had to buy in to those goals in the first place. The company was not paying her for her opinions. One of the new realities in the workplace is that our opinions actually add very little value. If you are using your expertise to critique ideas, point out the pitfalls of every plan, and the weaknesses of others, you are holding your company back. Top value comes from being able to deliver despite these challenges, not from pointing them out.

To succeed, your buy-in is not optional, and action, not opinion, adds value. Either find a way to get your mind around your organization's goals and sign up, or transition yourself to another organization. There is no third option to stay and hate, resist, or loudly critique. In this chapter, I outline the five new realities you must understand in order to buy in willingly and create value not through opinion but through action. Embrace them, and invest in your own future as well as that of your organization. Deny them at your peril.

Five New Realities You Can't Afford to Ignore

Reality #1: Defense Is the First Act of War.

If you find yourself at war often, know that your reactions are to blame. Even if someone else starts a conflict, you have the power to diffuse or neutralize it. People waste so much of their energy on defense and resistance. Your level of Personal Accountability should remain constant, whatever your circumstances. By editorializing on decisions made over your head, you squander what influence you have. You can always have an impact on your situation—as long as you first accept it.

A woman who had been promoted to a leadership role told me that she thought she was sufficiently bought-in to the goals of her organization because she unfailingly implemented plans that came down from upper management, but during our coaching session

125

she was shocked to realize she was actually holding her team back by voicing dissent: "I used to do whatever the company wanted me to do, and let everyone else know they had to go along, but I would come right out and tell my colleagues if I thought it was a bad idea. When I realized what I had been doing, I was so embarrassed. The company pays me to deliver a message and I'm not doing it! I'm editorializing and giving them my personal opinion. So now, when people in my team say the vice president doesn't know what the hell he's talking about, I say, 'Let's go talk to him!' People back down immediately. We don't always know the whole story behind what we are being asked to do, so we need to focus on our own jobs. Get used to it or get over it! I've learned that what you say counts as much as what you do, and if you don't buy in someone else will—and they'll achieve the goal first."

One of my clients told me that, in her office, a lot of people tend to focus on the negative side of new initiatives. When they were given a financial goal to meet last year, they all thought it couldn't be done. "I asked my colleagues, 'How should we accomplish this?' And it was crickets in the conference room. Kiss of death. I had to admit, I didn't know the solution, either. What we all kept thinking about were the barriers to our goal. So we decided to talk about those. We wrote down twenty reasons why it would never work. Not all of them had an easy fix. But then we changed our conversation to how we could—not why we couldn't—and we saw four solutions we could implement without too much hassle. We started with those. We built a nice sense of momentum for tackling the tougher jobs, and now we are on track to meet the goal. And we got here by turning our natural tendency to negativity to our advantage."

It's unlikely you'll ever encounter a risk-free strategy or perfect decision. There are no guarantees—every plan entails risks. That's why it's so vital that you are proactive in planning for what might go wrong and coming up with ideas for how to succeed anyway, because we all know that circumstances are apt to change without warning.

The value you add is identifying potential problems and fixing them with the minimum drama possible. Anticipate outside conditions that might interfere with your team's success—and create strategies to overcome them. All plans have risks, but when you step up and willingly mitigate those risks you ensure any problems that arise will never reach your clients.

Reality #2: The Most Valuable People Say "Yes" the Most Often.

Quickly accept plans and ideas of others. The most powerful words in your vocabulary are "Sure," "Yes," "Of course," "Glad to," "Appreciate the opportunity," and "I'm here to help." If you are tempted to say "No" and resist, what motives can you find? And how's that working out for you? You may say we want "balance" or to "set boundaries" when the truth is you are scared and unwilling. People think that saying "Yes" is the soft option. (Consider the pejorative term "Yes man.") I would like to convince you that saying "Yes" is the more courageous and difficult thing to do and should command our respect. It involves dropping your ego and surrendering to something bigger. Your energy will flow freely if you get wholehearted about what you're asked to do. If you feel underutilized or bored in your current job and want to move up, saying "Yes" as often as possible increases your influence. When you say "Yes" to something, you improve your ability to influence any situation. When you fight it and say "No," you have dropped out—you no longer have any say in what happens. You aren't going where the future of your company is going. Start from "Yes." Quickly recognize and radically accept your reality and channel your energy to moving forward instead of burning calories coming up with reasons and excuses not to. You will be so far ahead of everyone who is spending two hours a day arguing with their reality. What could you do with those two extra hours? Just say "Yes," already and quit holding out. You are only holding out on yourself.

Reality #3: Your Opinion Has Been Replaced by Google (but We Still Need Your Expertise).

A huge issue in workplaces is that people express discord, even pain, when asked to implement plans that they didn't have a say in. People truly seem to believe that living in a democracy means that their opinion should count on most things, and they become very upset when they are not asked. While input from highly accountable people can and does have value, most people's opinions are not valuable because they focus on why things can't be done, or why all action should stop until risks can be averted, circumstances perfected, and success guaranteed. Your organization does not need that kind of input. It needs talent that can move forward and succeed in spite of imperfect plans and circumstances. The value you add is not pointing out why a plan won't work, but finding ways it can. Profit is made by moving forward, not by opinionating on the perils of considering moving forward.

You should approach your work the way you do your commute. When you drove to work today, did you stop at stop signs? Were you infuriated that the city planners didn't take time to ask you whether or not each individual corner merited a stop sign, given traffic patterns? Or did you simply follow the instructions and stop at the stop signs without expending a ton of extra energy being upset that you weren't consulted? If you have been insisting on being consulted over issues at work as a condition for your support, there is a flaw in your logic. Resist the urge to react and get out of your lane. Instead, conserve that energy and stop at the stop signs at work with joy, or at least neutrality, rather than misery.

There is a hierarchy of opinions in most fields of endeavor. So why should your field be any different? The short answer: It shouldn't. Decision-making theory has proven that a strategy called satisficing,[1] in which we look for the "good enough" plan is more expedient than optimizing (seeking the "best" plan) or consensus building. Studies have shown that putting a ton of time, talent, and opinion into an initial decision has very little impact on the final outcome. Yet optimizing or consensus building are what we are often asking our companies to do. Since we can't be sure what is the "best" plan, and people are unlikely to come to a consensus on it, we are better off implementing any plan with diligence and mitigating risk along the way. The bigger and less cohesive the group, the more true this is. It's not personal; it's just that we have all been replaced by Google. (And thank goodness!) There are so many sources of great ideas—many of which are based on research, experience, and evidence—that our opinions just aren't as valuable as they once were. Opinions are based on personal preferences, not expertise and measured results of what has worked.

Information is so freely available that the value is no longer in influencing what to do. It is in execution. Picking a best practice at random to be implemented by a great team (you) is genuinely more effective than consulting everyone first. You are going to have to adjust as you go and stay light on your feet no matter what plan you're implementing. So get grateful that you don't need to be involved in decision making and become a genius at making things work.

You will only become frustrated and Emotionally Expensive by making your opinion known in a situation where it isn't called for.

You will also shut down the lines of communication just when they need to be open. Julie, a communications director, used this advice recently with good results. Her organization was in the middle of a two-year strategic planning process. They had finished the review phase and would soon begin implementation. Julie's boss called her in to show her the plans, on which Julie had not been consulted. Julie later told me, "When I saw the plans, I wasn't keen on the way they were structured. I work for a consensus-based leader, and usually I do feel that she values my opinion and I feel free to speak up. However, this time was different. During our meeting to discuss the plans, her tone let me know that she was looking for my buy-in, not my feedback." Julie picked up on her boss's expectations immediately and was able to modify her approach. Instead of giving her opinion or complaining about the plan, she made it clear that she was on board and then said she had some questions to ask to clarify her role. Because Julie's boss could see she was already committed to implementing her plans, they were able to have a much broader, more open conversation than they might have had. Julie said, "I got a lot of information that would help me do my job as communications director. I also began to really see her logic and the thought she had put into the plan. After our conversation, I ended up feeling confident that it would work even though it wasn't the way I'd have done it."

If you are not the decision maker, if no one asked for your risk/benefit analysis, give your leaders and coworkers the gift of getting over it. Most people are there to catch the wind, not decide which way it is blowing. Many times, we do not have all the information that the decision makers have, so we aren't in a position to judge. We also cannot expect to have input without accountability, which would only create chaos. There is a reason why the decision makers are in their position. If you want what they have, do what they did to get there. In the meantime, welcome the fact that you are not interrupted by being asked your opinion all the time. Adding your talent and effort postdecision makes a great impact. Stick to implementing with excellence and fine-tuning as you go if you want to add value.

Reality #4: You No Longer Have a Job. You Have a Role.

Those who work with me are sometimes shocked to discover that I am not a big fan of job descriptions. For me they mean very little. I hand them over with a list of caveats: This is my best guesstimate of what you might be doing for some of the time that you are here. But, basically, your job is to work toward the goals of this organization in every way you can, all the time. I draw a distinction between focusing on your job and your role. Your job description isn't the beginning and end of your responsibility. Consider how you fit into the larger goals of your company. Who are you there to serve? How can you make sure that happens? It's the difference between, "Sorry, that's not my department" and "Let me find someone who can help you." Your role is to do whatever it takes (within your licensure, your expertise, and the law) to delight the customer and deliver quality. The sooner you get clear on that, the happier and less conflicted and anxious you are going to feel.

I consult to hospitals a lot, and one of the ways you can tell if you are in a hospital that is running well is to ask for a blanket. In a hospital where the staff is aligned with the larger goals of their organization (to take care of people, to serve patients and provide comfort), you can ask anyone for a blanket and get one, no problem. In a hospital where things are not going so well, where people are all focused on their individual jobs and agendas, ask the wrong person for a blanket and instead you will get a lecture about

131

why it is not their department and you have to go ask someone else. What's your organization's blanket? What is the thing that every person, regardless of their job, needs to be able to provide for the customer? Every person who works there should be able to step outside his job, if needed, to fulfill that request.

When you act as if you own your company, you give the gift of your work unconditionally. You care about making everyone look good, not just yourself. You contribute generously to the whole, not just your part, and you have a clear line of sight to the organization's strategy at all times. You recognize the difference between your job description and your role in that larger picture, and you focus on that role as your true assignment. Your goals will be aligned with that of your organization—there's no conflict of interest. You don't expect anyone else to do that which you are unwilling to do yourself in the service of the greater good, and you're willing to take some risks, within reason, to reach those goals.

To test whether you are truly bought into your organization's goals and fulfilling your role in the larger picture, think of how you feel when customers are let down by their experience, regardless of your personal performance or contribution to that experience. How bad do you feel, on a scale of 1 to 10? How far would you be willing to go to correct their impression?

I can always tell hospitals that are headed for trouble because when I go in to do employee surveys, employees are very focused on themselves and their own needs and wants. We get feedback like, "We need the hospital to pay for our scrubs," and "We need better parking" and "It would be great if there were pizza in the break room on a Friday." All the feedback is self-focused. Whereas, in hospitals that are successfully delivering great patient outcomes, the focus is on efforts to improve patients' experience. Their employees might ask for help streamlining the bureaucracy or increasing accuracy. Their responses show that they are looking to serve rather than be served, and it makes such a difference not just in patient care and profit but in their morale. People who are focused on serving do not have time to think about the pizza they are not eating on Fridays, and as one consequence they are happier. They are more engaged. They are also doing a better job at their jobs. We all have a financial stake in our companies that goes way beyond our paychecks. If you want your organization to survive and thrive, you owe it to yourself to bear that in mind.

Reality #5: Resistance Is Not the Same as Feedback.

Resistance often comes in the form of your opinion that you disguise as "feedback" after the decision has been made but before you have stepped up and applied your talent to the problem. What it says about you is that you are unwilling or incapable. Be careful not to disguise any opinions or resistance as feedback. If a decision has been made, opinions are no longer welcome. Postdecision, highly valuable employees just get willing and get to work.

I know this frustrates some of you, but we need to clarify what feedback is. Feedback comes from credible witnesses whose data is recent because they have been on the front line, trying to make it work. They're trustworthy because they're completely willing and wholehearted in their efforts, not sabotaging. Feedback is for after you have said yes, made the effort to get something done, and brought back data from your experience of the project—for example, how you could do it faster, better, or cheaper next time. Feedback keeps the action going.

If you want input into future decision making, deliver amazing results. Get so skilled that you can play your role in a variety of scenarios, not just your preferred scenario. Then your leaders will come

133

and study you to see what you're doing right. Your influence will grow. Your job is to focus on how it can be done rather than reasons why it can't, or shouldn't. In case you're wondering, I give the same advice to the corporate leaders I coach. Believe it or not, this element of working life never goes away. If anything, the higher on the ladder you climb, the more important this piece of advice becomes.

Wholeheartedness: The Antidote to Fatigue

A complaint I hear a lot out on the road is, "I'm tired, Cy. All this talk about stepping up is hard for me to think about because I'm exhausted all the time. It's not that I don't want to make the effort, but who has the energy for something extra?" Now, I've got a two hundred speech per year schedule. I'm on a plane every other day. I've got eight sons at home. I know what tired is all about, believe me. On the average day, though, I feel energized, and so can you, regardless of how much you have to do.

The reason you are so tired all the time is not your workload, it's your approach. You are wasting too much energy on resistance, half-heartedness, avoidance, procrastination, and dread. If you doubt it, consider what happens sometimes when you leave work, longing only for sleep or television, and on your way into the house you get involved with something you love instead. You spot some weeds in the garden, and before you know it, two hours have passed happily digging away, still in your suit. Or your kid comes up to you with a basketball, and you're back in action. What happened to that fatigue? It was dissolved by wholeheartedness. The same approach works at work. Why not try it? Jump in, get on board, surrender to what is being asked of you. You'll get high energy and great results for your company.

134

I promise that if you get wholehearted about each thing you do, you will find energy and excitement about your life that buoys you through your day. If you can't get out of something, get into it. Once you come to this resolution, you will see resistance itself as the "extra" thing you don't have the time and energy for.

Focus on the Big Picture

No matter what your role in implementation—however small or large—all you do must contribute to the big picture, and it's all too easy to lose sight of that when you're focused on your piece of the puzzle. Always be thinking about what you're doing in terms of how it serves the larger organization and whether you are pulling your weight.

So, what did I tell that IT employee from the beginning of the chapter who had been arguing with the call to add value in a company with lofty IT goals but very few tech-savvy employees? Instead of belittling those she was hired to help, she needed to create training classes to teach basic computer skills. She needed to turn people on to online typing programs. She needed to use every opportunity to teach people, starting where they were rather than where she thought they should be. She needed to get her focus out of her own opinion and into selling her coworkers on the incredible features of their IT system that they could learn to use and grow their business. She needed to become allegiant to the goals of her department, fulfill her role, and channel her energy and talent to great strategies rather than strident opinions. Nothing less than that would make her wholehearted and successful.

If you get wholehearted, and commit to action over opinion, you will be on the leading edge of accomplishing your company's goals. The one thing that can scare people right off of that leading edge and back into resistance is change. Yet change is constant in every workplace and in every life. In the next chapter, I show you how to get fearless at change. Your competition won't know what hit them.

TAKE THE FAST TRACK BACK . . .
from Opinion to Action

Are you tempted to editorialize or offer your opinion?

Ask, "Am I using my opinions for good (to move the action forward) or evil (to stop it in its tracks)"?
If your motive is to stop the course of action or question a decision, change your focus from why it won't work to how you can help to make it work. Get willing, buy in, and use your expertise to mitigate the risks you see.
Make a list of the outcomes you fear, and how you can prevent them. Then think of three things you can do, right now, to move the action forward. Do them wholeheartedly, and be proud of your contribution.

7

Rule #4
Say "Yes" to What's Next. CHANGE IS OPPORTUNITY.

Here's an excuse that makes my heart sink every time: "I'm not very good with transitions/change/ambiguity. It's just my personality." I also hate "Change is hard," "We need time to adjust," and "It's all happening too fast."

Thirty years ago, *change capitalization* became a buzzword and the topic of countless seminars and books, and we're still talking about it. What other competency would you be given thirty years to master? My first presentation on this rule was in 1989. Saying you're no good at change is like saying to your company, "Don't waste resources or promotions on me! I'm going nowhere and loving it." Wait, did that sound harsh? Well, it's kind of like if your daughter's date knocked on the door carrying a 40-ounce beer and smoking a joint. "Hey, I can't help it, dude. I have an addictive personality!" How harsh would you be?

People have become ridiculously averse to even the word *change*—let alone the concept. I propose that you eliminate the word from your work vocabulary and skip the drama completely. Remain neutral and think, "Here's what's next." Our pain is not from the changes in our lives, but from our resistance to those changes. The minimum expectation is that you will not freak out when your cheese is moved. You need to start anticipating and capitalizing on the opportunity inherent in change, and moving toward it quickly and happily. It's not your boss's job to lead you through change. It's your job to get flexible and flow seamlessly into what is next. Let go of the idea that things should stay the same. Of course things are different. It's called progress and innovation—it's how you add value and how you get to be first to market.

The Three Stages of Change

There are three stages most of us pass through as we confront change: resistance, rejecting change out of fear and a desire to stay safe at all costs; maintenance, just surviving, doing just what we have to to support the change and no more; and vision, leaning into change, pushing for it, and making it happen. Most people tend to move through all of these stages as they come to terms with change, but in this chapter I make a case for going straight to Stage 3, vision, and making it your default mode when considering what's next. You'll learn how to get there by working on the four capabilities that visionaries share.

Visionary Capability #1: Be Prepared

Resistance to change is very expensive—it's a drag on the system. If you are one of the 20 percent of people who are chronically resistant, other people are going to eat your lunch. Your loss will be their gain, and there will be nothing unfair about it. Being bad at change can no longer be laughed off or excused as a personal idiosyncrasy.

Employers need flexibility and a commitment to change when it's necessary. Knowing this, why are so many employees so resistant to it? The number one reason is fear, though very few people are willing to admit it. It's hard to acknowledge that you doubt your ability to integrate new ideas, stay on top of technology, or adapt to new ways of doing things. I always say F.E.A.R. stands for False Event Appearing Real.

Anyone who has worked in an emergency room will tell you that most injuries from falls are the result of people's attempts to resist falling. It is common to shoot out an arm and then break your wrist, when what you ought to do is pull your extremities in and let your nice, padded torso take the impact. You may be bruised but your bones will stay intact. Resistance—when we dig deep and analyze our reasons—is usually about the desire for safety. Instinctively, when we are threatened with change, we take a defensive position. Actually, it is far safer to trust that you are able to handle whatever comes your way. Let your skills, your expertise, and the techniques you have learned in this book absorb the impact.

People who have a high score for Future Potential, who are developing more quickly than the demands of their workplaces or the market, are unfazed by change. Why? Because they live in a state of readiness. People who are ready step easily into what's next. If you have not done what you needed to do to stay current, then you are backed into a corner and your only option when responding to change is resistance.

Years ago, I was the head of a human resources department in a hospital. Our hospital was expanding, and the space available kept changing. As a result, some departments had to move around a lot.

Since it's a lot harder to move an ICU than an HR department, my staff bore the brunt. Our offices moved four times in six months. By the third move, everyone was really suffering. They couldn't find any of their stuff in piles of boxes, and there was a big gap between my expectations, which had not diminished, and their productivity, which definitely had. Meanwhile their story about the gap was that it was about my unrealistic expectations given the circumstances. When I wouldn't lower my standards, it became an increasing source of frustration. When the fifth move was announced, they came to me almost in tears and begged me to lobby my boss to let them stay put, much like most of us when we are in pain and ask our leaders to please change our circumstances. "Tell him we're not moving any more! It's not fair that no one is having to do this except us. What about our need to be productive and have stability to do our work?"

I was on my way to the boss's office to relay this message when, luckily, I ran into a mentor of mine in the hall. She said something to me that made me turn around and go straight back to my office. "Cy, do you really think that they are in pain because their offices get moved a lot? They are in pain because they haven't yet gotten mobile." I realized that even if we avoided the fifth move, our circumstances would remain subject to change. No one was going to guarantee us the same office in perpetuity.

I didn't ask my boss not to move us. I did, however, ask my team for a plan on how to get mobile—and it had to be budget neutral. I wanted to bulletproof them, to grow them beyond their current circumstances so they would be immune to changes in their reality. I called them to focus on solutions rather than bemoaning their circumstances, and they came up with a ton of great ideas for how we could adjust rather than reasons why we shouldn't have to. They traded our desktops with a department who hated their new laptops. They volunteered to be part of a pilot group that was testing out cell phones. They scanned their files. They got light on their feet. They made it so that we could go to any office and be up and running within five or ten minutes.

We got great at moving. We were so much more productive and effective because we could get out into the rest of the hospital and interact with the positions we were hiring for. We understood what people needed like never before, and we maintained our equanimity in the face of change. Once we embraced our circumstances and became accountable, and took action, not only did our results skyrocket, we all started working from home on Fridays, and no one even noticed. Don't victimize yourself by wishing for different circumstances—capitalize on change. Change yourself. Who knows what unforeseen benefits will come your way?

If you want change not to hurt, get prepared. If you aren't developing, change will expose your lack of competence, but if you are keeping up with your development, you have no need to resist. Your success will not be dependent on everything staying the same, but on your readiness for what's next.

Visionary Capability #2: Reframe

Mental flexibility is an essential attribute of a visionary. Reframing is choosing to see your situation as a great opportunity rather than a challenge or an assault, even when you aren't sure yet what the opportunity is going to be. Change can be stressful even when we're doing your best, and reframing will take the self-imposed part of your stress away.

One great way to reframe is to question what virtue your situation will help you develop so that you can improve. If fate lands you with an annoying intern whose foibles have stopped being cute, consider it your opportunity to work on patience. If your steak is too rare when you're out to dinner, practice courage in politely sending it back for more fire.

Another reframing technique is to see through people's behavior to their needs. People usually need your love the most when they deserve it the least. A manager raging about a dropped call is passionate about serving the customer (albeit in an Emotionally Expensive way). A coworker who is nagging you about a project deadline is probably getting pressure from her boss. She needs reassurance that you are on top of it.

A final technique is to reinterpret something negative as a positive. The continuous channel surfing of your spouse is just part of his curious nature and zest for knowledge—of what is on every sports channel.

Think of all the times in your life when, in the moment, you were sure what had just happened was terrible. Later, with hindsight, you could see that it was for the best. What if this reality you are so sure is wrong, were really perfect, and just the way it should be? And how could you know that it isn't?

My mother used to say, "It's all good in the end or it's not the end." I have been humbled many times by that bit of wisdom. At one point in my career, I was consulting with an international company that had approached me with a thrilling opportunity. I'd be working in Australia part time with an incredible team on a high-profile project. The offer was generous—they even threw in travel and lodging for my family whenever the kids had a break from school. I felt like I'd won the lottery. Then, just as quickly as the deal had come together, it evaporated. I was devastated—not just by the missed opportunity, but because I'd cleared my calendar and turned down other projects. I had three months ahead of me with no prospects for income. It was hard to see the upside.

Then, while I was in the process of regrouping, my mother was diagnosed with a recurrence of the cancer she'd had years before. Had the project gone through, I'd have been under strict contract and extremely limited in my ability to get home to see her. As it was, I got to spend my mother's last months with her and my family, and it was one of the best times of my life despite the sad circumstances. The truth is, we know very little about how things should work out, so we need to be open and trust that we are capable of handling whatever is next.

Visionary Capability #3: Give Yourself Permission to Fail

Early in my career as a therapist, I noticed that some of my patients, upon recognizing a negative pattern of behavior in their lives, would react by taking responsibility for it and working on new habits. Others would use that pattern to sew themselves a heavy coat of excuses that they'd wear forever. The latter group really frustrated me. To the forty-year-old who was still blaming his mother for his problems, I wanted to say, "She had you for eighteen years—you've now had twenty-two years to fix yourself. What gives?" Sometimes, though, something that is easy for others to see is hard to admit to yourself. I had an experience like that and gained a real awareness of how tough—and rewarding—it can be to break a pattern and change the script.

I wanted to be a runner my entire life. But I had gotten to middle age without ever trying it, and I was not sure I'd be any good at it. At least, this fear of failure became my story about why I didn't run. I idolized a young woman from my town who is a Nationals champ, and every morning, she used to run past my house. To me, she represented everything admirable about an individual: she was dedicated, hardworking, smart, nice—all that and fashionable, too, so I thought, "This is what a runner is." She gave me a very clear image of what I wanted to be. So every New Year's, I'd buy gear—new shoes, running magazine subscriptions, one year even a fancy stopwatch—the kind of things I was convinced it took to be a runner like my hometown idol.

When we want to make a lifestyle change, the first thing 80 percent of us do is go out and make a purchase. The odds are that the purchase, whatever it may be, is not going to lead to a lifestyle change. That is why we have garages, people. That is where we keep the Stairmaster and the Abdominator workout DVDs and the special bento boxes we bought so we could carry our fat-free lunch to work. The garage is where lifestyle changes go to die. So everyone except me can see I'm going about it all wrong, and in the meantime what I'm thinking—every year—is, "This year's going to be different."

It didn't get me any closer to becoming the runner that I said I wanted to be, because somehow it was the running part that eluded me. Until one day, a woman named Mary came up to me and said, "Cy, I can make you a runner." She teaches women how to run as adults, and she lives in my town, and she doesn't even want to be paid. "I'll pick you up at seven o'clock," she said, and I panicked, actually started arguing with her about why it wouldn't be possible, laying out my excuses. She said, "Oh, I see—you didn't really want to be a runner," and began to walk away, because Mary only works with the willing. I went after her and told her seven o'clock would be great.

The first morning, I asked, "How far are we going to run?" and she said, "Three miles." And I said, "I can't run three miles." And she said, "How do you know? How recent is your data? Did you already try it this morning?" I had to admit that no, I hadn't tried in over a year. "Then you have no idea—that's a mental issue." I said, "Well, I can't run it fast and I can't do it without stopping." She said, "We have a lot to work on here."

Mary started training me for a marathon, and I was nervous about a ten-mile run. She asked me if I could run one mile and I thought she was letting me off the hook for the day, so I was smiling. "Sure!" Then she said, "We are going to do that ten times." She never solved my problem for me, but instead helped me work on my mind, on my story that I didn't have the ability to become a runner. She got me to believe that I could, and then I did. I've run marathons, and those achievements mean a great deal to me because they did not come easy. The mental aspect was more difficult than the physical, which brings to mind my favorite running quote, from John Bingham: "The miracle isn't that I finished. The miracle is that I had the courage to start." I had to open myself up to the possibility—the threat—of failing. It was so much easier all those years to fold the new running clothes lovingly away in a drawer than it was to handle the idea that I might not make it around the block, that I wouldn't live up to my role model—an impossible standard that made it even harder to contemplate getting out there. The more a goal means to you, and the bigger a perfectionist you are, the harder this particular fear is to face.

A friend was scared to try running around her local park. "What if someone sees me? What would I wear?" Less than two years later, she had not only become a runner but completed the 155-mile Marathon des Sables, raising thousands for charity along the way. A personal trainer who helped her prepare used to say, "Don't fear perfection because you will never achieve it." This was very perceptive on his part. He could see part of her was holding back from pushing herself to the limit of her capabilities, scared to find out what those limits were. A lot of us so want to be perfect—whether consciously or subconsciously—that we are afraid to find out what we actually are. The irony is, what we actually are is something better: we're real. What do the people who love you love about you? I am willing to bet it isn't your perfection.

Give yourself permission to fail. Change means risk, and that's way too scary for people who are so in thrall to their egos or their unrealistic expectations that they don't see failure as an option. But the truth is that we all tend to overrate the risk of change and underrate the risk of maintaining the status quo. The cost of doing nothing is often higher. One way to move into vision quickly is to analyze the risk of what you fear will happen. If the worst-case scenario occurred, would it really have the impact you are imagining? Or is your story about it what scares you more?

Visionary Capability #4: Move On from Your Mistakes with Confidence

If you tend to beat yourself up for your mistakes, or feel uncertain or discouraged before you have even begun a task, you can be sure you need to work on confidence.

If you have been mired in Learned Helplessness at any point in your career—you may have come to believe things about your limits, or your working relationships, that you haven't tested or proved. You may have ideas about yourself that have nothing to do with who you are today and what you are capable of doing, ideas that convince you that you are incapable of adapting to something new. A limiting belief, if not examined and questioned, can solidify into a barrier that blocks your ability to see opportunity in change.

The competency that allows you to succeed in new circumstances comes after confidence, not before. Confidence is what you build through thinking: changing your mind-set and inquiring on untrue stories. Competence is what you then build by doing. So when you realize something is not working, or you have made a mistake, do what you can to fix it, leverage your learning, move on as quickly as you can, and do better next time. Don't let your failures become your identity—either in your mind or in the minds of others.

Leaders can tell who lacks confidence by the lists they get handed every time a new challenge emerges. We ask our leaders, "Got a minute?" They lie and say yes, then we let them have it: the list of what we need to rise to the occasion—more people, more budget, more time. What they hear is, "You perfect my world, and I will give you the gift of my work." That list of demands—what we need to do our jobs—is our "lack of confidence" list. It's the exact impulse that caused me to go out and buy vast quantities of running gear and then wear those clothes to sleep in and never go running. I thought I needed all that stuff to be a runner. Turns out that to be a runner, all I really needed to do was run.

Whether you believe something possible or impossible—either way, you will be right. So, work on your beliefs, grow your confidence. Set an intention to lean into every opportunity—especially the ones that present themselves as problems, the ones that make you annoyed, make your palms sweat and your heart race. Recast that feeling of fear as excitement and adrenaline. And desist with the lists. You can do this. In Rule #5, I show you how to make the mental leap over common excuses and barriers to success and succeed anyway.

TAKE THE FAST TRACK BACK . . .
from Resistance to Vision

Are you resisting change?

Ask yourself, "What am I afraid of? What am I protecting or defending?"

Be ready for what's next—work on skills and development before you need to.

Reframe your situation as an opportunity.

Don't let fear of failure stop you from trying. Let go of the emotion and look at the risk analytically.

Everyone makes mistakes—own yours, then move on quickly and confidently, applying what you learned.

Believe that whatever is happening is happening for your highest good.

8

Rule #5
You Will Always Have Extenuating Circumstances. SUCCEED ANYWAY.

If you are anything like the people I teach one on one, in seminars, and in large group lectures, you will have been taking the Reality-Based Rules in, one by one, nodding and thinking, "That makes sense. Choose happiness.... Ditch the drama.... Add value . . . simple instructions . . . I get it." It all sounds so sensible, and in a perfect world you would get right out there and get started. Who doesn't want to raise their value, deliver great results, and be happier at work? But your world is messy, and this isn't going to be easy. That is when the hands go up, and you start to question everything. Before you head back out into your real lives to put the rules to work, you want me to know I have no idea what you are up against. You're right—I don't. But I do know one thing: Your reality is not the reason why you can't succeed. It is the circumstances under which you must succeed.

In Part One, I said that the ultimate freedom comes from being able to succeed in spite of your circumstances, unbeholden to others for your success. Benefits in work and life come to those

149

who deliver results—they are not incentives to encourage you to deliver. Those who deliver results become very influential because constraints are not going anywhere. Your time and resources will always be limited. You may have heard that, of the attributes "fast," "cheap," and "good," at most you get to pick two per project. In my experience, this is usually true. High-value players are able to move with agility within the dreaded triple constraint. You will encounter many snags in your reality, but the snags you need to worry about are the ones in your mind-set and your approach. Those are the ones you can affect.

There are two paths at work: the one to success and happiness, and the one to reasons, stories, and excuses. If you practice the first four Reality-Based Rules, you will either get the results you were hoping for, or you will learn something that will help ensure you will be successful in the future. You will certainly reduce your Emotional Expensiveness—and boost your value to your employer. If you don't follow the Rules, you will end up with great stories about why you couldn't succeed, why other people are wrong, and you're right. But you won't get the results you want, and you won't be happy. This is the anti-excuse chapter, where I'm going to share some of the most common barriers I hear about, and show you how you can, and should, overcome them. I know you can do it because others are out there doing it every day. They have problems and extenuating circumstances, too, and it's not stopping them. So, what's your excuse?

Excuse #1: My Boss Is a Jerk

If you're thinking, "My boss shouldn't be a jerk," or some similar judgment about any person or situation, you're telling yourself a story. The worst thing you can do is make up a story, believe it, and stress over it. We all spend too much time trying to figure out what's "right" in our own humble opinions. The truth is that we are seldom truly called on to make a moral judgment. Is it really true that your boss shouldn't be a jerk? Does it matter, given that statistically, you are unlikely to get a perfect boss more than once in your career? Bosses come in all the varieties that humans do, and you will have good and bad bosses. What's good about the bad ones is that you get really competent at managing yourself. "I shouldn't have three new bosses within a year" becomes "I'm flexible, I'm learning new management styles, it's entertaining." If you have ever acted like a jerk, or done a job inexpertly yourself, you should be able to identify with his or her plight. So, ask what you can do to make things run smoother in the office. Figure out your simple instructions—the next thing you can do to add value. Action with impact leads to joy. Inertia hurts, so surrender to your circumstances and find the opportunity instead of using your energy to fight, complain, or resist.

High-Value Players Change Their Beliefs, Not Their Bosses

Be rooted in the idea that the universe is benevolent and everything that is happening is happening for your higher good. One of the ways to express this is by trusting others in a professional context—this shows your confidence in them and in yourself. This is especially true when it comes to your leaders. Leaders have a responsibility to act with integrity, consistency, decency, and respect. And I can guarantee you that every leader will fail you at some point in your relationship. That is reality—they are human, too. If we are basing organizational trust on the perfection of our managers, that is a fragile prospect indeed. Trust is a choice that professionals make based on their faith in their own competencies and abilities. It has little to do with the other person's integrity or trustworthiness and everything to do with your courage. People who trust themselves to make good choices have a high level of trust in others.

If you believe that you can't work well for a bad boss, you are limited to only being able to succeed with a great boss, and I don't like those odds—they are not in your favor. If your boss is really bad, and you are considering calling the employee hotline to lodge a complaint, or making a visit to human resources, first make absolutely sure that your complaint is really about your boss and not a lack of accountability on your part. Ninety-nine percent of calls to employee hotlines are just people blaming others for their circumstances, essentially confessing their own incompetence. They will complain about their reality, and ask for it to be changed, but they won't know their real problem. What might that sound like? "Uh ... I don't like working for a boss who holds me accountable for my work so I'd just like a new one, please." Most of the time, pain comes from a lack of accountability.

If the problem with your boss is that the boss plays favorites—and you're not currently one of them—why not get busy figuring out how you can turn that around? It isn't just your boss. The world plays favorites, too; it's called a market. So get used to it, study what those favorites are doing, and become one of them.

When you are finding the opportunity in your latest challenge, you will know because you'll be stressed very little. No one can change your circumstances. The only way out is through, so change your mind-set. Instead of, "My boss sucks," try, "My thinking about my boss sucks." There are things you can change, and things you can't. Part of being based in Reality is knowing the difference between the two.

Excuse #2: My Coworkers Are Difficult/Bullies/Rude/Indifferent/ (Insert Adjective Here)

At work, you have to spend a lot of time working closely with people you didn't choose. This leads to conflicts that may have you spending far too much of your time worrying about what is and is not under your control. I'll give you a shortcut: you are the only person whose behavior you can change. When faced with a challenging situation, look first to yourself. Take a quick inventory of the things you are doing that may have exacerbated the situation and what you can do to ease it.

Shortly after I spoke at a hospital, a new member of a team of nurses was transferring a patient from her unit to another unit in the same hospital, and she phoned the head nurse for the shift to let her know she would bringing the patient downstairs shortly. The head nurse was a bit rude and impatient with her, and she became nervous. Had she done or said something wrong? The transfer went poorly. The head nurse was peremptory with her and slammed the patient's chart down on the desk. She could sense the patient's anxiety. He felt as unwelcome as she did. She left him reluctantly and retreated to her unit upstairs.

She wanted to share her story with the other nurses on her unit—to get validation or sympathy for her bad experience. But instead of spreading the pain around and starting what she knew would quickly blossom into a story about the other unit's rudeness and unwelcoming attitude to patients, she did something different and, she later said, wholly out of character. She tended to be shy, so this took a lot of courage. She picked up the phone and dialed the head nurse. She said, "I just noticed—and I think our patient noticed—that you seemed really frustrated and upset just now. I'm just wondering what I could have done—what I should do in the future—to ease the transition between our two units?"

The head nurse was disarmed by her willingness to help and to take accountability for their difficult interaction. She was also surprised at how she had been perceived—she'd been so busy and stressed on her shift, she hadn't realized the impression she was giving and she apologized. She then went to apologize to the patient and make sure he had everything he needed. It was a complete turnaround. Relations between the two units became cordial and transfers go smoothly, thanks to one person's willingness to deal directly with the problem instead of telling a story and nurturing a grudge.

High-Value Players Confront Coworker Conflicts

"How can I help?" is the one question that will put you on the fast track to resolving conflicts with others. Tattoo this on your body and ask it often. Listen carefully to the answer you get and go do that. Avoid gossiping or going to your supervisor to complain when you have not made an effort to be part of the solution. It reflects poorly on you and it erodes the trust among colleagues. Ask yourself how you would like to be approached if the situation were reversed, and offer your colleague the benefit of the doubt. What I have learned is what I teach: Be quick to forgive, because next time it may be you who needs to be forgiven. See others with generous eyes.

Unless there is a clear-cut case of bullying, or a real power differential, you are better off resolving the situation directly than taking it to your boss, complaining to others, or creating a triangle of any kind: you know, those times when you are tempted to tattle or gossip instead of confronting the issue head-on. If you find yourself talking to others about the person with whom you have a conflict more often than you talk to that person directly, you are making the problem bigger, and yours is fast becoming the greater crime. It may not come naturally to you to confront, but if you do it calmly and in the spirit of being part of the same team, you will be more likely to get a positive response and have the favor returned. That kind of give and take—without ego or defense—is a hallmark of effective relationships both inside and outside the workplace.

Excuse #3: My Team Is Really Dysfunctional

Our jobs would be so much easier if it weren't for other people, right? Here's where we're lucky: team dynamics are not innate. You can—and should—work to strengthen and improve them. When you are struggling while working in a group, keep in mind this counterintuitive truth: Most conflicts do not come from personality clashes. They come from lack of clarity.

People tend believe conflict is inevitable and invariably personal. This isn't true—it can't be, or no one would ever get anything done except in a perfectly matched team. I spend a lot of time teaching people not to personalize conflict, because conflict isn't about personality differences. Instead, we need to professionalize it.

The root cause of conflicts among people is ambiguity in goals, roles, and procedures. You can get the smartest group of individuals in your company together to execute on a plan, and if they can't get clear on these three fundamentals, it will descend into name calling (at least the mental kind) within days, if not hours. If you have these three things clear, there is no such thing as "personality conflict." You can work with anyone.

Before you start a new project, while you're getting to know the other people you'll be working with, check in with them about what your common goal is, who is doing what, who is the decision maker and what roles the rest will play, and what the first steps will be. This is not about taking over or trying to get people to do things your way—it's a collaboration. You can't assume that other people know what your role is, or that you all have the same goal in mind. You may need to ask questions of your supervisors if you find your group is not clear on goals. If you need to clarify your mission, or what to prioritize, make it plain that you are bought-in and willing, and that the team is eager to move forward, so everyone will know that they can count on you. This should effectively close the door on colluding and complaining within the group.

If you begin a project with different goals (spoken or unspoken), it will only lead to frustration and conflict as you try to formulate your procedure. Of course, sometimes you will have to work with people whose desires are different from yours, and negotiate a compromise. It is in these situations that we are most in danger of seeing success as a zero-sum game and butting heads over who will "win." We are used to thinking about competition in a very limited way, but if you want to be able to negotiate strongly and keep it cordial, don't be afraid to put your competing interests on the table for discussion.

Draw a box and label it *OR*. Above it, write your shared goal—the one that transcends this conflict. On the left and right sides of the box, write your point of conflict—each person's individual desire.

Inside the box is where your solution lies. Cross out the *OR* and write *AND*. Think in terms of both/and rather than either/or and focus on the bigger goal at stake. If you are still in conflict, make sure you are clear on what that larger goal is—only then can you find a solution that respects both of your positions. Anytime you are stuck in *or*, you are doomed, and victimhood is yours. If you want to step up and step out of the box, if you want to win, try making it a win-win instead of a contest of wills. Find the huge power that resides within the simple word *and*.

High-Value Players Respect and Nurture Team Dynamics

Although success requires individual traits like gumption, initiative, and resilience, its ultimate expression can only be realized in the context of a team.

Your organization needs a team player far more than it needs a star. A lot of people are surprised when I say that a team player is often more valuable than a star. Whereas a star might have an inflated sense of his contribution, value independence over making it work, and expect to be asked his opinion before he joins the effort, a team player says "Yes" early and often. A team player builds on the accomplishments of others and shares information rather than hoarding it to protect his position. A team player raises the bar for everyone and knows that success is not a zero-sum game. There is more than enough to go around. Team players compensate for one another's shortcomings. Even the most technically accomplished person will become a drag on productivity if he or she can't work with a team.

Team players care about making everyone else look good, too, so they offer help and share their best practices freely. In return, they get a lot of loyalty and their teams function better. A client who manages a large retail store stated very simply, "We all want to be helpful in some way and we don't want to be yelled at. I go to work and strive to help people, be nice, get the job done, celebrate the ordinary and have some fun." His approach contributes to a culture of contentment and productivity. So much so, that when he took another job, many of his coworkers went with him, some even taking lateral moves. Those who stayed behind "still keep in touch. They help me, and I still help them."

Being a team player is not about being a martyr who gives to a fault and never asks for anything in return. On the contrary. You will find the rewards of being a team player outweigh the effort. You will find your voice amplified and people willing to do favors for you because you have been generous and upstanding to them. The point is that if you want something for yourself—be it a raise, a promotion, a better shift, or someone to cover your vacation—the way to get it is to think in terms of what the team needs and not what you need. Act as a partner—high impact and low maintenance. There is nothing going on in your world that is not co-created by you, so if you want great results, start with a great mind-set and give other people the benefit of the doubt.

A client, Leslie, was having a real conflict with her team: "As a senior member of a design team, I'm expected to contribute a high level of creativity. I felt that the other people on the team didn't contribute as much as I did, and they didn't understand and appreciate my contribution. They were always asking me clueless questions that only proved how little they 'got' my work." Leslie had decided that her team did not understand her and was acting on that story. This allowed her to play the role of the misunderstood creative genius—and conveniently ensured that she didn't have to take responsibility for issues that arose within the team or for the team's overall results. She saw her results as separate from those of the team as a whole. But in reality, she was holding back from sharing her process or collaborating fully with them, and their work was suffering. What a huge turnaround—Leslie figured out that she was the one misunderstanding her team's needs. She went from considering herself the victim to owning the issue and being able to resolve it.

A mentor of mine introduced me to a tremendously effective concept: "That which is missing from this situation is something I am not giving." When you find something missing (especially—but not limited to—intangibles, like honesty, generosity, humor, sensitivity, or gratitude) don't dwell on what other people "should" be doing or giving. Change your terms to increase your serenity and efficacy. Be the change you wish to see. You go first. When Leslie began to show respect to her team, she got respect in return. When she started to communicate more freely with them, their questions became more relevant to her creative process. By the same token, if you want support, give support. If you want openness, be open. If you want cooperation, be cooperative.

Most of the time, this works. It isn't about controlling or manipulating others but about changing your own approach. Even if others don't respond to you in the same spirit, you will feel less stressed, with the peace of mind that comes from knowing you have given your all. There is no need for stress, because being kind and supportive and helping is our natural state and when we are doing that, we are happy and empowered. Let's do the things that make us feel great at work—and in life, for that matter. You will be working to your highest potential, not the lowest common denominator.

Excuse #4: The Culture at My Company Is Hostile/Toxic

A lot of times I hear, "Cy, I would like to implement your rules, but it wouldn't work at my company. Everyone would need to be on board, and the culture/leadership/et cetera is not open to it." Some people think that if they are to become Reality-Based, and follow the Rules, they need support from HR, or they need their leaders to share the philosophy. But when people talk about the "toxic culture" at their organizations, what I hear them really talking about is their shared reasons, stories, and excuses for their lack of results.

A company's culture may take years to turn. This has long been used as an excuse for not trying to change anything within a company. But within the larger culture are microclimates—anywhere you find ten to twelve people working together—that are far easier to change. It's like buying air-conditioning for your house because changing the weather is not an option. Your working environment is up to you and the others working in your immediate vicinity. So get started changing that.

I've seen it all in terms of bad workplace situations, and sometimes bad things happen to good employees. You still get to choose how you respond. I once worked with a group of people who were shutting down a factory where they had worked for years. They decided to make the best of it—even as they worked themselves right out of their jobs. Knowing they were about to be unemployed, they chose to see it as their chance to shine, to write their own story. They acted as if their final weeks were a job interview in themselves. In fact, some of the factory's former employees were so proud of the way they had handled the closure with integrity and poise that they based their job searches on that story. They found that, even a down economy, if companies are hiring, they want people with the ability to stay positive and committed in adverse conditions. They got new jobs, and they proved that you can create a great climate, even in the worst situation.

High-Value Players Know When to Walk Away

It is important, whatever happens, to know your worth—not just the dollar amount of your salary but your worth as a great employee and a human being. You are more than any job. If you are doing the things I advise in this book and they are not working, it may be that you have a bad fit where you are and it's time to move on.

So how do you know when it is time to leave a job, boss, or situation? This is not a simple answer; it has more to do with what is going on inside of you than what is going on in your company. We tend to attract what we project. Now, before you think I am blaming you for the problems of others, hear me out. People often blame the macro (culture) for why they aren't happy in the micro (their jobs). But we are all responsible for our own happiness in the micro. Rule #1: Happiness comes from Personal Accountability. It is only when you find a way to be happy in the micro, in spite of your circumstances, that you can take full advantage of whatever macro you find yourself in.

Here's a simple example. Say you live in a small town and you would prefer to live in a big city. If you go to New York from a place of resenting your small town, you will not automatically find the happiness you seek. Whereas if you have lived life to the fullest in your small town, and practiced accountability, and connected with others joyfully, you will be the sort of enlightened and self-mastered person who can feel truly at home anywhere. You will be ready to fully enjoy New York when the time comes.

If you are in a work situation you believe is toxic, know that all workplaces have a level of toxicity. Not everyone is Reality Based; not everyone is accountable, and there are bullies out there. There are suboptimal circumstances everywhere. So what you need to do, to answer the stay versus go question in a constructive way, is come to a place of neutrality within yourself.

The problem isn't really stay versus go. It's that you must not do what I call "stay and hate" or "go and blame." If you do either of these things, you will not be able to flourish in the job you're in, or your next job. Instead you need to learn what you can where you are, and be so accountable that you mine the situation for every possible lesson. The problem for many people is not their toxic environment but their inability to be assertive, or their inability to stick it out through some discomfort until they reach a point of equanimity: "I could stay and do this—with joy, even—but I prefer to go and do something else." Once you have learned what you need to learn with fluency, and are satisfied that you are thoroughly Reality Based and accountable for your own happiness regardless of circumstances, you are in an ideal position to leverage what you have learned in a new job.

If you do make the decision to leave, you will know you have tried everything and be confident that you're not simply running away from difficulty and taking your problems with you. If you stay, make it a conscious choice and not a passive one. Do it joyfully. Stay and serve, or go in peace—there is no third option.

The way you handle your reality—your particular set of circumstances—will either boost your value to your organization or kill your chances. Throughout this book, you have gained insight into a revolutionary, more enlightened, and strategic way of understanding your true value. Instead of wishing your circumstances were different, start wishing you were different. Make yourself over in the Reality-Based image and your life will change for the better. When you are based in Reality, all of your relationships improve. It doesn't just work at work. You can't change the world, but you can change the part you play in it. If you create peace and sanity in your home and in your working life, you will attract more of the same.

TAKE THE FAST TRACK BACK . . .
and Succeed Anyway

Are you feeling stuck?

Look for ways in which you are co-creating your problem.

Change your beliefs about what you need in order to be successful.

Confront conflicts early, calmly, and in a spirit of teamwork.

Ask, "How can I help?"

Get clear on goals, roles, and procedures.

Think in terms of *and*, not *or*.

You go first—give that which is missing in any situation.

Call to Action
Put the New Rules to Work

W hat if that worst-case scenario is sounding all too familiar right now? A number of people who have attended my seminars have admitted, mostly after the fact, that their introduction to my material was tinged with a sense of embarrassment and growing recognition. They saw themselves in it—and not in their best light. If this describes you, if you realize that you have been less than Personally Accountable in the past, or Emotionally Expensive, you may be concerned about how to change in the context of your daily work. My best advice is to let your actions speak for you. If you commit to being less Emotionally Expensive and more Personally Accountable, and start making choices and acting from that mind-set, soon enough people will see a difference. At that point, if you wish, you can mention that you are working on changing some things.

If it makes you feel any better, most of the highly successful executives I've coached have had times like this at some point in their careers. One of them told me, "When I was younger, I was a chief offender. Somewhere in my late twenties, when I started to manage people, I realized I had to make a transition because I was so drained all the time. I couldn't imagine continuing to live with that level of drama. I became less emotionally attached but I lacked a structure. When I came across your material, I thought, 'Here is how work should be.' You provided a framework for how I could focus on my passion for my work, help change the culture at my company, and drive everyone's energy toward a common purpose." It's never too early and it's never too late to make this transition.

Here's what to do: Figure out the one thing that, if you get better at it, will improve your outcomes and enable you to take more action. Get busy working on that. Action with impact leads to joy and happiness. Movement begets movement. It can even become perpetual. So stop swimming against the current; surrender, and use your energy for impact. Dare to become a curve-breaker.

Avoid overpromises or big announcements. These changes are about progress, not perfection. If you are human, you will screw up, but only hourly, so forgive yourself. You can practice new, Emotionally Inexpensive responses silently to yourself until it feels natural. You might find yourself answering questions differently or starting conversations in new ways: "In the past I might have said X, but I've been rethinking my approach and now I think Y." It's a recalibration that will happen over time, and as it does you might find yourself seeking out a new crowd at work or making some new friends.

What if you already are a curve-breaker who has been reading this book, wishing that other people would finally get it? Judgment can be a real pitfall of top performers, and it's one of the main ways people who are highly productive bring down their numbers without realizing it.

One of my coaching clients admitted she and her colleagues had succumbed to judgment at what was otherwise a moment of triumph for them. "We were getting kudos from the CIO and the CFO of our company, while the group that used to complain we were too slow now complained that they couldn't keep up with us. Once you become Reality Based and start to see great results, it is a real temptation to look down on others who are not doing as well, and that is exactly what we were doing. We had to stop ourselves and realize that we are not in competition with people in our own company. We're on the same team. We should be helping them catch up and sharing what works for us and how we got so effective—not getting cocky about it."

Her self-awareness is really refreshing, and it's something we can all stand to develop further. There's ample reason to quit judging others for your own sake, but everyone around you benefits. When people feel blamed and critiqued and judged, they become defensive and cannot work to their potential. They won't take risks. They might even shut down and contribute nothing. If someone in your organization is not performing at the level that he or she can, ask how you can help. You are all in it together, so consider their struggle your struggle, too.

One of my readers who works at a university has been committed to the Reality-Based Rules for some time, and she's enjoying her results, but she is often frustrated when others don't match her level of productivity. She said, "I'm more valuable to my boss because I'm willing to put my personal agenda aside for the team, and I'm not a contrarian. I had a boss once who said that good work is rewarded with more work, and that is definitely the case in my job. In higher education you rarely get merit-based promotions or raises because the money isn't there. So I look to other indicators that my performance is strong, and I've chosen to see my boss's reliance on me as a sign that I'm performing well. But how do I avoid the tendency to want to judge others or feel entitled?"

What if you put in the effort to become Reality Based and highly productive and others don't work as hard as you do? What if "they" don't promote and reward you? Here is the worst-case scenario: you will end up happier and more skilled than they are. It's not a bad risk. You'll be prepared to take your show on the road if that's what you choose. Forget fair versus unfair. Very little about the world is fair. If you think you shouldn't have to work harder than everyone else, you're right. But would you rather be right, or happy? If your goal is to be happy and free, simply do what works—for you, for your organization. Stay in your lane and make an impact; be the most valuable and resilient person there.

Better yet, use social pressure as a force for good. Social pressure is strong, and sometimes just understanding that the majority are moving in one direction makes others decide to follow their lead. A group of researchers went into hotels that use "Please reuse your towels" signs. They changed one of the signs to read, "Most people in this hotel reuse their towels at least once during their stay." Immediately, towel reuse rates went up 25 percent, and laundry bills went down.[1]

Find visionaries, like you, who are willing, and focus on them. Then go after easy converts among your coworkers in maintenance. Personally invite them to join your group—call them up to greatness! As for those in resistance, who are negative, don't do their share, or don't care, forget about them. There will always be a few in every organization, but their numbers are small and they can't bring you down without your permission.

Once you have your group of visionaries working together, don't let yourselves become the silent majority. Speak up for your own viewpoint, and keep the action moving. Once I was facilitating a meeting in which my job was to introduce some changes to the structure of an organization. Immediately, a few people spoke up to critique the changes and their leadership team, and the tone of the meeting quickly became negative. I remained calm and firm, thanked them for their input but did not allow the meeting to stall. I asked people to remain professional and supportive, and as I spoke I could see quite a few people in the meeting were nodding. From my place at the front of the room, I got a sense that the majority in the room were in favor of the changes that were happening.

The meeting ended, and as I headed to my car, my phone started buzzing with text messages from people who'd been in the room. In all, more than twenty people texted messages like, "Cy, I totally agree with where we're going." And "Know that I supported you and loved what you were saying." I appreciated their support, but had they spoken up in the meeting, it would have saved a ton of time, thwarted the resistors, and I wouldn't have had to bear the brunt of the resistance alone. As it was, the few people in resistance were able to leave the meeting thinking that they were in the majority. After all, they'd been the ones doing all the talking, and they hadn't seen how many of their colleagues were nodding their silent support. So my message to the visionaries is, Speak up! Stick up for your positive viewpoint—no need to judge or attack the resistors or become self-righteous about it. Just don't allow the few to stop the action of the many or affect the atmosphere with their negativity. One of my favorite stories about focusing on the positive and ignoring the negative is that of a grandfather teaching his grandson about life.

"A fight is going on inside me," he says to the boy. "It is a terrible fight between two wolves. One is evil—he is anger, envy, sorrow, regret, greed, arrogance, self-pity, guilt, resentment, inferiority, lies, false pride, superiority and ego." He continues, "The other is good—he is joy, peace, love, hope, serenity, humility, kindness, benevolence, empathy, generosity, truth, compassion, and faith. The same fight is going on inside you, and inside of every other person."

The grandson thinks about it and then asks his grandfather, "Which wolf will win?"

His grandfather replies, "The one you feed."

If you are stressed and unhappy, you are feeding the wrong wolf. You are probably focused on the past or on stories—not reality. Get accountable and focus on the facts, the future, and what you can do to affect it, and you will be a high-value player who is on the fast track to success and happiness.

If you get Emotionally Inexpensive enough, you will become a value generator for others. Just as Emotional Expensiveness is multiplied because it affects others, Emotional Inexpensiveness can help to change others' attitudes and neutralize their drama.

Raising your value with the New Value Equation won't happen overnight. Be prepared to get this book out daily as you practice the five Reality-Based Rules. Applying them is a process that will take place over months and years to come. You will mess up. You will have mulligans and do-overs and return again and again to the Rules before you internalize them as habits of mind and action to help you boost your value and become happier at work. It's worth it, so don't give up. Look for support, extra content, free webinars, and like-minded people on my website, www.realitybasedrules.com.

Your company needs more people like you—you are the drivers, and you are developing capabilities that are all too rare in the corporate world today. In years to come, I hope to be writing about employee-led turnarounds in companies everywhere. It all starts with you, as you work to fortify your current performance, guarantee your future potential, and decrease your Emotional Expensiveness, becoming a high-value player who is as inspiring to others as you are valued by your organization.

Reality-Based Employees' Manifesto

We ...

1. Give the gift of our work freely and joyfully
2. Are clear that suffering is optional and often self-imposed
3. Don't see buy-in as optional
4. Work in challenging circumstances and succeed anyway
5. Conserve the energy that many put into drama and use it instead to have impact
6. Would rather be happy than right
7. Understand that our happiness is correlated to our own level of accountability
8. Support organizational goals and decisions even when we weren't consulted
9. See reality not as the reason we can't succeed, but the circumstances in which we must succeed
10. Are inner directed and accountable
11. Seek out feedback and take responsibility for our development and our future
12. Understand that there is no "third option"
13. Study and emulate the successful
14. Say "Yes" to what's next—and mean it
15. Find the opportunity in every challenge

16. Focus on the follow-through, not on our egos and opinions
17. Ask, "How can I add the most value?" and then go do that
18. Instead of judging, ask, "How can I help?"
19. Know that actions rather than opinions add more value
20. Are quick to forgive and see others with generous eyes
21. Own our outcomes, enjoy the positive, and learn from the negative
22. Document and share our knowledge
23. Believe that everything happens for our higher good
24. Are clear that the mind-sets and actions that lead to our own happiness are the very same as those that produce great results for the organization
25. Answer the call to greatness, no matter what the source

Notes

Introduction

1. American Psychological Association, *Stress in America 2009*. Retrieved from http://www.apa.org/news/press/releases/stress-exec-summary.pdf

Chapter 2

1. http://www.marshallgoldsmithfeedforward.com/
2. Lombardo, Michael M., and Eichinger, Robert W., *The Career Architect Development Planner* (Minneapolis: Lominger, 1996), iv.

Chapter 4

1. Miller, John G., *QBQ! The Question Behind the Question: Practicing Personal Accountability at Work and in Life* (Kirkwood, NY: Putnam Publishing Group, 2004).

Chapter 5

1. Katie, Byron, *Loving What Is: Four Questions That Can Change Your Life* (New York: Three Rivers Press, 2003).

Chapter 6

1. Simon, Herbert Alexander, *Administrative Behavior: A Study of Decision-Making Processes in Administrative Organizations*, 4th ed. (New York: Free Press, 1997).

Call to Action

1. http://greeneconomypost.com/7-ways-employees-change-greener -16772.htm

Acknowledgments

I have always suspected, and now am completely convinced, that the universe is profoundly kind!

Here's a bit of my proof—those who have blessed me with their talents, gifts, and love.

Richard, thank you for making all my dreams come true. I wake up every morning stunned and thrilled that you have chosen me. Your heart is kind, your support unwavering, and your love is life altering. So glad we found each other again this lifetime.

Doris, thank you for loving my father and my family. You are a wonderful example of what love and faith look like in our daily lives. Having you at Dad's side gave me the peace of mind needed to write this book.

Terry, I am so grateful for your dedication and loyalty. Having you as my big brother and my boys' uncle has given me the courage to take the world by storm.

George, Charles, Henry, and William, you four are my pride and joy. I find myself simply in awe of your brilliance, wisdom, talent, kindness, maturity, worldliness, and limitless support for me. Thank you for doing far more than your share, holding down the fort, loving me from afar, and welcoming me home each week with bear hugs, smiles, and love. Love you to Pluto and back.

Harrison, Grant, Tyler, and Adam, thank you for taking me into your family and for sharing your father with me. I appreciate your patience and support as I have disappeared from time to time to work on "the book." I adore you all and love you a ton. I cannot wait to begin our life together on the lake.

Sara, you are a miracle worker and a godsend to me. Thank you for your amazing support and your enduring belief in me and our work together.

Jason and Greg and the team at Quantum, I so appreciate your genius and expertise as we have developed our work on accountability and created Reality Check. Engagement may be broken but we are well on the way to fixing it.

Erin, once again you have made magic happen from across the sea. Your ability to put words to my ideas is remarkable. You are the poster child for Personal Accountability—your willingness to do whatever it took in the writing of this book and your resilience throughout the process are the reason this book exists and can help millions of readers get happy again at work.

Giles, Karen, John, and the Jossey-Bass team, thank you for another opportunity to take the Reality-Based Revolution to the people. I am so grateful for your support, feedback, suggestions, edits, and calls to greatness, not to mention the many phone calls regarding the unnamed book! Once again, your team led the way in creating a great book with my name on the cover.

And finally, thank you to my clients who have wholeheartedly adopted the Reality-Based Rules of the Workplace and were so willing and anxious to share their incredible success stories used throughout this book. They are absolute proof that suffering is optional, success possible, and happiness readily available regardless of your current realities.

About the Author

Cy Wakeman is a speaker, blogger, consultant, and human resources thought leader. A sought-after conference headliner, she also delivers more than a hundred keynote programs annually. Cy has honed her Reality-Based Leadership philosophy as a consultant to top executives and organizations seeking to thrive in difficult times. For more than two decades, she has consulted on talent development with major clients in manufacturing, banking, government, high tech, and health care, including Bayer, New York Presbyterian, National Institutes of Health, Hospira, Hallmark, Federal Reserve Bank, Weil Cornell, Verizon Wireless, U.S. Cellular, TD Ameritrade, ConAgra, Omnium Worldwide, First National Merchant Solutions, Wellmark, Wells Fargo, Cabela's, Farm Bureau, and Trinity Health Systems. She has been featured in the *Wall Street Journal*, the *New York Times*, the *New York Post*, and on SHRM.com. She is also an expert blogger on FastCompany.com and Forbes.com. In 2010, Cy published *Reality-Based Leadership: Ditch the Drama, Restore Sanity to the Workplace, and Turn Excuses into Results* (Jossey-Bass).

She lives with her family in Omaha, Nebraska. For more information, please visit www.realitybasedrules.com.

Index

181

W

Y

Z